Jumping Hurdles

Jumping Hurdles

Steve Brown

A Raven's Ridge Book

Baker Books

A Division of Baker Book House Co.
Grand Rapids, Michigan 49516

© 1992 by Steve Brown

Published by Baker Books
a division of Baker Book House Company
P.O. Box 6287, Grand Rapids, MI 49516-6287

Trade paperback edition published 1997

Previously published in cloth by NavPress under the title *Jumping Hurdles, Hitting Glitches, Overcoming Setbacks*

Printed in the United States of America

Library of Congress Cataloging-in-Publication Data
Brown, Stephen W.
    [Jumping hurdles, hitting glitches, overcoming setbacks]
    Jumping hurdles / Steve Brown.
       p. cm.
    "A Raven's Ridge book."
    Originally published: Jumping hurdles, hitting glitches, overcoming setbacks.
Colorado Springs, Colo.: NavPress, 1992.
    ISBN 0-8010-5768-X (pbk.)
       1. Consolation—Meditations. 2. Encouragement—Religious aspects—
Christianity—Meditations. I. Title.
    BV4905.2.B729 1997
    242—dc21   96-40524

To
Launia Cole Brown,
whose wisdom and love enabled me
to overcome many setbacks in my life

CONTENTS

IN PREPARATION

I know a woman who left her family. She was distraught, lonely, trapped. Her husband was beside himself. He fussed with her, pleaded with her to return, questioned himself, wondered why all this was happening. She didn't come home. He kept agonizing over why. She wouldn't tell him. Finally, he went to her and reached out. She was surprised and overwhelmed.

One of the advantages of being a Christian is that we're free to deal with life's hurdles in new and creative ways. Jesus gives us that power, that creativity. It's not innate and it's not always natural. And we don't always know how to explain it or why it works the way it does. This woman couldn't account for it. Her husband was certainly not sure why he went to her. But God knew and He was in charge.

The God of the universe allows those hurdles to come into our lives so we can experience Him in our midst. They're meant to teach us: We *can* jump those hurdles; we *can* act with God's power in ways that we've never known before; we *can* overcome life's hurdles, glitches, and setbacks. Why? Because Christ is in us.

This book is a series of meditational thoughts on this central fact— Christ in us. The topics cover a wide spectrum, touching on the areas of life that, if we're honest, concern most of us most of the time. Scriptures are offered along with meditational questions or reflective exercises. Sometimes I'll explain a Bible passage; other times I have chosen to let you just ponder God's Word, confident in the fact that the Spirit works quite effectively without me.

You can use these meditations as daily or weekly devotionals, or you can dip into them at your leisure or time of need. However you use them, my hope is that they will give you some guidance as you hit life's unexpected, often trying, and sometimes scary tough times.

Even today you'll face all kinds of hurdles, glitches, challenges, riddles, and setbacks; maybe they'll come in your own life, or perhaps in your son's or daughter's, or maybe in your spouse's. They may seem insurmountable. Or they be tiny glitches that only challenge for a moment or two. But they will come—that's a fact.

And God wants you prepared for them. Not so you can perform for Him or for others, but so you can listen to Him and grow in Him and strengthen your ability to serve others for Him. If you listen or read between the lines of life's fine print, you can hear God whispering, talking, and sometimes shouting, "I am here! All is well." He wants us to overcome life's challenges, and the best way is His way. And how do we do that? By listening, by being creative, by keeping our perspective, by acknowledging His ways, by remembering Him . . . and sometimes by godly actions that surprise us but never surprise Him.

That's what this book is all about.

PART • ONE

JUMPING
HURDLES

He had worked long and hard to get to this place. His daily routine was a challenge for even some of the more experienced athletes, but he was determined to have a winning season. So he listened to what his coach told him to do and did it.

He ran a couple of miles, warming up with the cross-country team. Then he'd do calisthenics with the sprinters. Sometimes he'd run up and down the stadium stairs with the weight lifters. Then would come working on his technique exploding out of the blocks, so when the starting gun would fire he'd already be ahead of the other runners. Of course, he also had to strap on ankle and chest weights and run—for clocked time—several 100-, 220-, and 440-yard dashes. Then, with only ten minutes or so of rest, he'd begin work on his technique for jumping the hurdles. One day he tried to determine how many hurdles he had jumped in any given week. When he got to over four hundred, he quit counting.

But now, this day, at this race, he knew all the hard work would finally pay off. Out of all the hurdle runners in his state, he was one of the six fastest. Today, he would compete against his rivals. Today, he wanted to prove that he was the best. His coach believed in him, but he never gave him a sense of false pride. Indeed, his coach had more faith in his ability to win than he did.

"Ready," shouted the starter.

This is it, he thought. *Remember the basics, don't get cocky. Think about what you're doin'.*

"Get set," came the second command.

My stomach's churning so much. That's okay. It's nervous energy you can use. Now concentrate. Give it all you've got. And don't forget the basics!

Dead silence. Eternal-like silence.

BANG!!

He fired out of the blocks. The race was on.

Do you ever feel like you're in a race? You are, you know. The apostle Paul often talked about the Christian life as a running race (1 Corinthians 9:24-27; Galatians 2:2, 5:7; Philippians 2:16; 2 Timothy 4:7). And it's not an easy race. Life's track has bumps, curves, and lots and lots of hurdles. More hurdles than you can count or even see. The bumps are minor irritations. The curves are more serious; sometimes they're difficult to maneuver, and they can slow you down. However, they too can be handled with even natural skills. But the hurdles—they're a different matter altogether.

In order to jump a hurdle without knocking it over or hitting it hard enough that it will slow you down or throw you out of the race, you need some training, some expert guidance. And like every skill, you must start with the basics, learning them until they become like your shadow—inseparable as long as you're staying in the light.

The basics of the Christian life are not as many as you might think, but they're essential if you're going to run in life's race. And let's face it, as long as you're alive on planet earth, you're in the race, whether you want to be or not. The question isn't, Will I run in the race or not? You're already in it. Rather, the issues are, How well will I compete? and Can I win the race? The answers to those questions are entirely dependent on your willingness to master the basics.

So that's where we'll begin—with the basics. But remember now: You can't learn them overnight. You must practice them daily, routinely, methodically. Your Coach will have it no other way. I know. He's still working me because I still forget them sometimes. But I'm grateful He's patient and He has more faith in me than I have in myself because He knows . . . well, I won't go into that now. That's one of those basics I was telling you about.

Go get on your running gear. The workout is about to start.

CHAPTER ONE

KEEPING
OUR
PERSPECTIVE

Do you not know that in a race all the runners run,
but only one gets the prize? Run in such a way
as to get the prize. Everyone who competes in the
games goes into strict training. They do it to get
a crown that will not last; but we do it to get a crown
that will last forever. Therefore I do not run like
a man running aimlessly; I do not fight like a man
beating the air. No, I beat my body and make it my
slave so that after I have preached to others, I myself
will not be disqualified for the prize.

Paul the apostle
1 Corinthians 9:24-27

The Ways (and Needs) of a Man

Before you can run in the race of faith, you have to be a part of the track team. That means you need to decide if you want to make the commitment to become a member of God's everlasting family, for only they make up the runners of faith. Perhaps you've already made that decision and count yourself among God's family. That's great! But if you're unsure, or you know you're not and you want to be, then listen up. This chapter is for you.

In 1 Peter 2:21-25, the Apostle Peter reminds us of what God has done for us in His Son, Jesus Christ. But it's up to us to respond to this incredible message of hope. As an honest searcher, do you long for forgiveness yet realize that you can't forgive yourself? Are you striving for something more, believing that life ought to be better and different? Life can be richer, more meaningful, truly different. But not on your terms. If you really want something better, you must start with God. How? Peter's words will tell you. Let's consider them carefully.

First, note the prominence Peter gives to the concept of human sin: "He himself bore our sins in his body on the tree, so that we might die to sins and live for righteousness; by his wounds you have been healed. [Of what? Of your sin.] For you were like sheep going astray" (verses 24-25).

When I was in high school and college, I had a dance band. And even though I was a pagan then, my band always closed our dances with a song, "He." The song's closing words were, "He always says, 'I forgive.'" To this day, I don't know why we sang that. Perhaps because it was a nice melody, people enjoyed dancing to it, and it made us feel more spiritual. Whatever our motivation, the song made no real difference in our lives.

Perhaps your concept of God makes no real difference in your life either. If it doesn't, you have the wrong God. If you believe God is sweet and saccharine, that God won't punish, that God is some kind of celestial bellhop, forget it. That's not the God of the Bible. It is a dreadful thing to fall into the hands of the living God (Hebrews 10:31). " 'For my thoughts are not your thoughts, neither are your ways my ways,' declares the Lord. 'As the heavens are higher than the earth, so are my ways higher than your ways and my thoughts than your thoughts' " (Isaiah 55:8-9).

God the Creator places a demand of perfection on His creatures: "I am God Almighty; walk before me and be blameless" (Genesis 17:1). Jesus affirmed this when He said, "Be perfect, therefore, as your heavenly Father is perfect" (Matthew 5:48). When God demands perfection, righteousness, obedience, and justice, He wants exactly that. No excuses and no exceptions. And He always gets His way. As the Sovereign over all, He is the highest court in the universe, and someday everyone will stand before Him to give an account of the way they lived. "Be sure of this: The wicked will not go unpunished, but those who are righteous will go free" (Proverbs 11:21). "For every living soul belongs to me, the father as well as the son—both alike belong to me. The soul who sins is the one who will die" (Ezekiel 18:4). If you think you're going to walk into the throne room of God carrying your offense against Him, you're wrong. If you think God is going to accept you the way you are, you're also wrong.

Do you know what sin is? Sin is all the arrogance of an alley cat spitting in the face of Almighty God. Sin is taking your life and your soul, which belong to Him, and using them for yourself. You may be saying, "Well, I'm human. I make a few mistakes, but I'm reasonably good." You're simply missing the point.

Sin separates you from yourself. Are you having trouble sleeping at night, tossing and turning, and you can't deal with it? You've got a sin problem.

Sin separates you from other people, too. Are you always smiling, trying to be loving, sweet, kind, and pure? Then at night, when you look in the mirror and take off your mask, do you know your image doesn't reflect reality? You've got a sin problem.

More importantly, sin separates you from a holy and righteous God, the One who is the only source of meaning and joy in this world. And you can't bridge that gap apart from Christ.

Second, Peter gives a prominent place to God's remedy for our sin problem: "To this you were called, because Christ suffered for you. . . . He himself bore our sins in his body on the tree . . . by his wounds you have been healed" (1 Peter 2:21,24). Through Peter, God is saying, "I have taken your sin problem and placed it on My Son. You're now free, pure, and righteous, not because you are yet, but because He is. Every time I look at you, I'll look through Him."

Suppose you had killed a man. You knew you did it—you were mad enough—and you knew all the evidence was against you. Called before the judge, he condemns you to death. Imagine further you had a friend who came into the courtroom and said to the judge, "I love my friend. I want to die in his place. I want to take his penalty upon myself." That's what God has done. "Christ redeemed us from the curse of the law by becoming a curse for us" (Galatians 3:13). "But we see Jesus, who was made a little lower than the angels, now crowned with glory and honor because he suffered death, so that by the grace of God he might taste death for everyone" (Hebrews 2:9).

Third, the Apostle Peter gives a prominent place to our response to God's action: "So that we might die to sins. . . . For you were like sheep going astray, but now you have returned to the Shepherd and Overseer of your souls" (1 Peter 2:24-25).

Jesus said, "Whoever comes to me I will never drive away" (John 6:37). God is a gentleman. He won't strong-arm His way into your life. He won't push and shove. Instead He gives you the freedom to make your own choice about Him. You can continue with the playthings of an empty, bored life and die, or you can follow Him and live. God comes into the darkness of our lives offering light. God comes into our loneliness offering eternal friendship. God comes into our sin, offering forgiveness. God comes into our death offering life. All we have to do is take it.

If you're out in the desert and dying of thirst, the water won't jump into your mouth, even if you know where it is. You have to go to the water and drink. Accept the Father's gift. Go to Him. Tell Him how you feel. If you don't know how, then in the silence of your heart, pray with me:

Father, I have sinned. I confess before You that, because of my sin, I'm separated from You and from Your plan for my life. I admit I have made a mess out of my life. I have tried to put it together myself and it just doesn't fit.

I know You sent your Son to die on a cross in my place,

20

to make me free and alive. Because of what You did for me in Christ, I want to be Your disciple.

Father, I ask now that You will make that transaction. By faith, I trade what I've got for what You've got; I trade my sin for Your forgiveness; I trade my emptiness for Your fullness; I trade my lostness for the eternal life You offer.

Take control of my life. By Your grace, make me Your faithful disciple to my life's end.

If you joined me in that prayer, you're a new member of God's everlasting family. Let me be the first to say, "Welcome to the family!"

TIME TO DRAW AWAY
———— ✤ ————
Read Psalm 68:1-6, Galatians 3:26–4:7.

For meditation:

If you just trusted in Jesus and became an adopted son or
daughter of His family, you've also joined His track team.
That imagery of faith's journey is well chosen,
for while the benefits are staggering,
the workout and race are filled with challenges. But know
that the Lord will never let you run alone: He will be with
you always, and He has provided the other members of
His family to come alongside you and provide support. So
begin looking for a church to plug into and let them teach
and guide you into the fullness of the faith
God has for you.

If, however, you've been a believer for some time,
turn to the Lord and praise Him for all He has done for
you in His Son. And realize that you haven't even begun to
enjoy all the benefits that will be yours
for eternity. So much is yet to come—I can hardly wait!

Relief for the Runner

Are you frustrated at work? Discouraged in raising your kids? Do you feel like you just can't keep on keeping on? Contrary to popular opinion, God is not in the business of making you miserable. We get discouraged all on our own. So the question we need to answer is, How should we deal with our discouragement?

For the Christian, life is a race we either win or lose. In other words, there are no second places. And if you are going to run in this race, you need to know some things: how to play by the rules, how to pace yourself, where to run, and how to run. Above all, you need a good coach. The writer of Hebrews gives advice from the best coach around—the God of the universe—and His counsel concerns how we can keep from getting discouraged while running the race (Hebrews 12:1-3).

Our Coach's first piece of advice is simple to understand but sometimes hard to do: *To fight discouragement in the race, we need to be unencumbered.* "Let us throw off everything that hinders" (verse 1). What does this include? What should we unload? Hebrews mentions two items, either one of which tend to cripple us or at least greatly slow us down.

One of these items is weight. When you're training to be a runner, you wear weights on your legs to build up the muscles. Once the muscles are strong, remove the weights and you just fly! That's the word picture the writer of Hebrews apparently has in mind, but he doesn't use it to convey something positive, as building up your spiritual muscles. No. What he's talking about is removing those weights that are keeping you and me from running the race of the Christian life as we can and should. What are the weights that are holding us back, slowing us down, even making us ineffective in the race? The weights are whatever hinders our faithful witness, makes us discouraged, and keeps us from standing strong. These things need to be cast aside.

What is your weight? It may be drinking. If that's a problem with you and your witness, cast it aside. Your weight may be a relationship that hinders your witness, or it may be your wealth. (There's nothing wrong with being rich, but sometimes money has a way of eating its way into your heart.) Your weight may be intellectualism, a love of food, perfectionism, or religiosity. Whatever it is, throw it off, cast it aside. And don't wait until tomorrow. Start today, right now. If you need help, seek it out. If you need prayer support, ask God to help you find it. But get radical about ridding your life of the weights that create so much unnecessary struggle and pain in your life.

We're not only to drop the weights that encumber us, we also need to get rid of our sin (verse 1). Using the imagery of the race, the writer of Hebrews says sin is like trying to run in a long robe—it clings closely to our legs and tangles us up, tripping us as we're trying to run.

I remember one time when I was in high school, about three o'clock in the morning a group of us decided to go swimming at the pool of an exclusive club at a hotel in my hometown. It was dark when we sneaked up to the parking lot and climbed over the gate. We got to the pool unnoticed and had a great time swimming—for about five minutes. Then one of the guys jumped off the high diving board sitting on a big inner tube. When he hit the water, he created a sound like a shotgun blast. It echoed so loudly against the side of that hotel that lights started going on everywhere. We all ran, except for this one guy. When I looked back, I saw him dragging the huge inner tube behind him, slowing him down, sometimes tripping over it. I yelled, "Man, drop that dumb thing. You're going to get into bad trouble."

Our sin is like that inner tube; it hinders our running, it dogs our steps, it trips us up. Sin will always weigh you down; it will discourage you and make you depressed. Lying, adultery, and stealing will do that. Greed, lust, and bitterness will also do that. Whatever your sin, throw it away, purge it from your life. The Lord will help you if you'll depend on Him. And He'll often use other believers to be His caring arms and listening ears. But believe me, if you get serious about abandoning your sin, as you see it fall away, you will be surprised at how much faster you can run.

Our Coach's second piece of advice is also vital: *When we're discouraged in running the race, we need to remember that we're both inspired and led by Christ* (verses 2-3). As our elder Brother, Jesus has gone before us. He has gone through everything we will ever face, and

He has faced it successfully. He has asked only that we follow Him.

When my family and I are in Tennessee, we like to visit the famous caverns in Townsend. Going way back under the mountains, those caverns are frightening places. They are dark, cold, and dangerous. But when you go down with a guide, it's okay. Like a pioneer who has blazed the trail many times before, he's very familiar with the caverns. He knows where to step and when; he knows what passageways lead to dead ends or are too dangerous to travel; he knows the ways in and out of those underground natural tunnels; and he's willing to take and protect any who will follow him. Our pioneer Jesus is like that. Having gone ahead, He knows what paths to take and which ones to avoid or to travel on with care. And He too will protect us. All we have to do is place our feet in His footprints.

The third piece of advice from our Coach is this: *When we're discouraged, we should not forget that we're also ruled in love* (verse 2). A British diplomat was sent into a very difficult territory. When asked if he was afraid, he said no, for two reasons. "First," he replied, "I represent the greatest power on earth. And second, if I get into trouble, all of that power, the power of the Queen, stands behind me."

It is frightening to know that you're running a race in which you aren't sure how well you run. It is also frightening to know that the race is for eternity, and there is no second place—only winners and losers. But the fear and discouragement of it all get better when you realize that the One who built the stadium in which we run; the One who made the rules for the race; the One who judges the winners and the losers; the One who decides when the race is over . . . is our Brother who loves you and me. Relief for the runner is all provided in Jesus Christ.

Someone tells the story about a British soldier whose courage broke during battle. Unable to handle his fear and the violence anymore, one night he ran from the front-line trenches. He hoped he could make it to the coast to catch a boat back to England. After a number of hours groping in the dark of a moonless night, he realized he was totally lost. The cold and his own fear had also gripped him. Finally, still trudging around in the night, he ran into what he thought was a signpost, but it was so dark he couldn't see what it said or which way it pointed. So he climbed the signpost and struck a match. In the glimmering of that match, he looked square into the face of Jesus Christ. Startled, he tried to collect himself and soon realized he was looking at a wayside crucifix.

Then he remembered the One who had died for him, who had endured, who had never turned back no matter what the odds. Though it took all the energy he had left, by the time the sun broke over the morning's horizon, he had returned to the trenches.

As a runner, when you're tired, afraid, and discouraged, the best way I know to get your second wind is to strike a match in the darkness and look on the face of Jesus Christ.

TIME TO DRAW AWAY
───── �֎ ─────

Read Hebrews 12:1-12, 1 Corinthians 9:19-27.

For meditation:

Are you depressed? Discouraged? Afraid? Exhausted?
Perhaps your load is too heavy.
What's weighing you down? Could some of the weight
be sin needing forgiveness? Our loving Father longs
for you to come to Him for cleansing and healing.
Or perhaps your focus is in the wrong place. Are your eyes
firmly fixed on Christ? Is He the One you
rest in and trust unreservedly?

Take some time to search your heart and look into the face
of Jesus. Confession is good for the soul; it lightens the
load and makes the race much easier to run.

Defining Your Identity

A few years ago I was asked to speak at a retreat just outside the Detroit area. It was one of those occasions when I really wanted to make a good impression. I admired several people there, so I felt it was important to do well. I know. That doesn't sound very spiritual. If I really loved God, I wouldn't be hung up on impressing people. Nevertheless, that's how I felt—and yes, I've already confessed it.

At any rate, I worked very hard preparing for the retreat, to make the teaching really good. I wanted to look good too, so I took my best suits. When I arrived at the hotel, the site of the retreat, as I met the people I would be speaking to the next two days, I made every effort to appear sophisticated and intelligent. To be perfectly honest with you, I think I made a reasonably good impression.

The next morning I was to speak for the first time at the retreat. But when I awoke that day, to my horror, I had lost my voice; I couldn't raise it above a whisper.

You've got to understand that God has given me a good speaking voice, and my voice is about the best ministry asset I have (aside, of course, from my wife, Anna). I have always felt that if I didn't have my voice, I wouldn't have much left with which to serve God. Someone told me once, "Steve, stay away from television, because you have the perfect radio face." I'm not good looking, I'm not brilliant, and I'm not especially pure, but I do have a good voice. When I was in high school, a history teacher told me, "Steve, you have a wonderful speaking voice. You be careful what you say, because when you speak, people will listen."

And so, there I was, getting ready to speak to a group of people I desperately wanted to impress—and all I could do was whisper. In all the years I've been a broadcaster or a preacher, I've never lost my voice. This was a brand-new experience, and it scared me to death. You see, I define myself by my good speaking voice.

So, I finally got serious with God, right there in my hotel room.

I confessed all my sins, made all kinds of promises, pledged my firstborn . . . if God would only give me my voice back. I told Him I was sorry about wanting to please people so much and that I would never do it again if He would just restore my voice.

Well, God had a different idea, and it didn't fit with mine at all. My voice not only didn't get better, it got worse.

I was panic-stricken, so much so that I couldn't hear God speaking. Panic times often blur out what God would teach us. It usually isn't until afterward that we're able to look back and see His presence and love. But if I had been able to calm my heart, I would have heard Him say, "Child, I have a wonderful surprise for you. If you will just be still, you are going to see something that you have never seen before."

And so I left my room and went to speak for the folks at the retreat. As I got up to teach, great fear still ruled my heart. I knew God had judged me for my sinful desire to please people and, further, I knew I deserved it. But I had forgotten about grace. I do that sometimes.

Then the most wonderful thing happened. As I whispered my teaching into a microphone turned up to high, I noticed that people were listening, really listening. Not only that, I noticed they were visibly moved by what I was saying. God was at work.

For the rest of that retreat weekend, I strained to even eke out a whisper. That glorious voice of mine remained packed away. Nevertheless, the weekend turned out to be one of the most meaningful and successful speaking engagements I have ever had.

After it was over and I was back home—my panic dissipated—I could hear the Lord again, and I began to understand the lesson He was teaching me. In effect He told me, "Steve, I have given you your voice, but I want you to know something that is much more important. Whenever I use you, it isn't *because* of your voice. It is because I have decided to use you. I am perfectly capable of speaking through a whisper just as much as a foghorn voice. Your problem is that you had learned to define yourself in terms of your voice rather than in terms of My love. You thought you were being judged when you were really being blessed—not because of your goodness but because of My grace. Try to remember that the next time."

I told the Father that I appreciated the lesson a lot, but suggested if He needed any advice, that He not take away my voice again in the near future. I reminded Him that I was getting older and that old people have heart attacks. He just laughed and told me to mind my own business. I heeded His advice, and I've learned a lot since.

I have mostly learned to define myself not in terms of what I do, but in terms of who I am. Better than that, I'm learning to define myself in terms of *whose* I am. The Father is teaching me that my value lies in belonging to Him, trusting His direction, and leaning on His grace. My value doesn't come from what He gives me to do but from who and whose I am when I do what He tells me. Put another way, I am valuable because I am loved by God, not because of what I do for Him. Jesus said, "I am the vine; you are the branches. If a man remains in me and I in him, he will bear much fruit; apart from me you can do nothing. . . . As the Father has loved me, so have I loved you. Now remain in my love" (John 15:5,9).

The trouble with most of us is that we sometimes forget we are defined by God's love, acceptance, and grace. Once we understand that and regularly recall where our true identity lies, what happens to what we do—whether we fail, succeed, change, resign, get fired, or are promoted—doesn't matter. We are God's own, His children, members of His everlasting family, the objects of His unconditional love. And He bought us with the blood of His very own Son, Jesus Christ. What else really matters? Nothing. Everything else pales into insignificance when compared to that.

TIME TO DRAW AWAY

———— ❖ ————

Read Psalm 145, John 15:9-17, 1 John 3:1-3.

For meditation:

Where does your identity lie? If it's in your children,
they will disappoint you. If it's in your work, it will wear
you out and leave you in the end. If you're looking to your
spouse for self-confirmation and affirmation,
he or she will fail you too.
Perhaps a position in your church or a spiritual gift
provides your identity, but those won't help you either.
Nothing in your world will ever really define you.

You must look outside, to the One who made You.
He knows you inside out, and He loves you
unconditionally.

Go to Him now, asking Him to help you
find your identity in Him.
He won't fail you, not now or ever.

Lessons from Pain

We have gone through a tragedy in our home. We have discovered that Quincy ("The Wonder Dog"), our German shepherd, has very serious congenital physical problems. Both of his hips are malformed, he has an overbite that prevents him from eating properly, and he has some other serious internal problems. Of all the dogs who have lived with our family, Quincy is the most loving. His love for our family is almost human.

I know. I know. He's just a dog. And most dogs with Quincy's problems are put to sleep, right? And I know animals are not created in God's image. I also know one must never over sentimentalize a pet. But Quincy has been a part of our household for almost ten months now, and, well . . . we like him a lot.

At any rate, Quincy has gone through the first hip operation, and it was very painful. He was with the vet (an experience that, before this operation, had been rather pleasant for him) for about four days, and during that time he was in incredible pain.

When we went to pick up Quincy, I was afraid his attitude might have changed toward me. After all, I took him to the vet and was, at least indirectly, responsible for his pain. If I had been Quincy, I probably would have been angry at the one who made me go through something that hurt me so much. And remember, as a dog, Quincy doesn't know that the pain is necessary for his healing. All he knows is that it hurts—a lot. Even before the operation, every time Quincy put any weight on that hip, he would whine. He could barely walk, and when he did, it was with great anguish. And so, with some hesitancy, we went to get Quincy from the vet.

Quincy looked horrible. He had lost weight. The two places where the surgery was performed (his hip and stomach) were shaved. He was obviously tired and looked far older than his ten months. But do you know what he did when he saw us? He started wagging his tail. He pulled at the leash held by the vet just so he could get next to us. And

30

when we got home, he came over and put his head in my lap—my lap! I couldn't believe it, but oh, how I enjoyed it. I petted him for a while and then gently pushed him away. He limped to the middle of the living room, turned around, and came back to me, once again putting his head in my lap.

Teacher and theologian Dr. Barnhouse once said that all of life illustrates Bible doctrine. As I was scratching Quincy behind the ears, I prayed, "Lord, make me like Quincy. I know You never hurt me without cause. I know You can't always explain why You do the things You do, but You repeatedly demonstrate Your love for me. Teach me to come to You the way this dog has come to me. Teach me to trust You and love You when it hurts, even when I don't know why I hurt."

I believe one of the reasons God is using Key Life, the radio broadcast I speak for, is because we are telling folks that God's love is the only constant in a changing world. You would think a simple message like that would be old hat. It isn't, and we have seen so many thousands respond to its depth and simplicity.

One of the elders in the church I pastored told me after a communion and prayer service, where the elders anoint people who ask with oil and pray for their particular needs, "Pastor, I never knew there was so much pain and so many problems in our congregation." I told the Father something similar after we started hearing from so many people across the United States. I said, "Father, I never knew there was so much pain." There is, you know. Saint Teresa once said, "Lord, You would have more friends if You treated the ones You had a little better."

When we hear from the great number of hurting people, I want to tell them that everything is going to be okay. But for some of them it isn't going to be okay, or at least it isn't going to be very soon. Sometimes I am tempted to say to them that they aren't exercising the proper biblical principles, or if I were especially manipulative, that if they would send a large contribution as an "act of faith," God would stop their pain and make their problems go away. Biblical integrity, however, simply doesn't allow that. If the perfect Son of God had to die on a cross, we must assume that crosses are a part of a fallen world, even when we're doing everything right.

Of course, God answers prayer. And yes, He changes circumstances, heals hurts, and makes things better. That's a part of our message. But sometimes the Christian faith is nothing more than keeping on keeping

31

on and trusting that God knows what He is doing and believing He does it "right well." Sometimes you have to tell people that when God doesn't remove the pressure, His love grants the power to endure the pressure. Sometimes you have to just trust.

Job cried out in his suffering, "Though he slay me, yet will I hope in him" (Job 13:15). In my study I have a banner my wife, Anna, made for me twenty years ago. It reads, "My Father, I don't understand Thee but I trust Thee."

And so I will keep telling people to go to the Father. I will keep speaking of His love, even when that love sometimes isn't apparent to those who hear the message. I will keep pointing to the Lord as the only One worthy of absolute trust. Someone has to face the pain and the hurt without giving out cliches. Someone has to point to God as the only resource of the believer.

Dogs don't need a lot of teaching. They naturally trust their master's love. Human beings are not always that smart. That's why God has given us each other—to remind each other of His love.

Go put your head in the Father's lap. You'll be surprised by His gentleness and His love, and after a while, He will take the pain away and make you well.

You can learn a lot from a dog.

TIME TO DRAW AWAY
——— ❖ ———
Read Psalm 91, Matthew 11:28-30.

For meditation:

How is God at work in you through hardship right now?
Can you bring yourself to accept the Father's love?
Would you place your head in His lap even now
and receive His care and compassion? He's longing to
wrap you in His arms and hold you close in His love.

The Greatest Fact of Life

There are facts, and then there are *facts*. That you are reading this book and that I am its author are facts. That God is in control of the world we live in and is its ultimate Author are *facts*. The difference between a fact and a *fact* is that life would not be without *facts*, but it could get along just fine without the other facts. One of the *facts* essential to you and me and the rest of the world is the *fact* of the resurrection of Jesus Christ. If the resurrection of Christ was not an absolute, space-time event—one of the ultimate *facts* of life—if, indeed, Christ is still dead in a grave somewhere, then the whole Christian faith is nonsense and our most central problem—sin—is still unresolved. The Apostle Paul put it this way: "If Christ has not been raised, your faith is futile; you are still in your sins" (1 Corinthians 15:17). The central *fact*, the greatest *fact* of Christianity, is that Jesus left His tomb alive, risen from the dead never to die again.

Perhaps you're wondering, "Assuming Jesus did get up out of the grave, what difference does it make?" It makes a lot of difference. It means that everything He said is true, that the teaching He gave is practical, that the mortal life He lived and the immortal one He now lives can make your life different now and forever. And if the dead man, Jesus, got up and walked away from His tomb, you can too. Like Him, you can live beyond the grave. This is why the whole superstructure of the Christian faith is built on the evidences for the resurrection.

"But," you might ask, "how do we know Jesus didn't stay dead? How can we be sure that He really rose from the dead immortal?" I want to give you a series of six questions whose answers lead to only one conclusion: an empty tomb and a risen Lord.

First, if Jesus remained dead, how can you explain the testimony of the disciples to His resurrection? If you had lived in the first century and had taken the time to look, you would have seen tears in the disciples' eyes at their leader's crucifixion. Everything they had worked for, prayed for, and slaved over died with Him, or so they first thought. If you had met the disciples at that moment, they would have explained, "We thought He was a King, but He died, saying that God had forsaken Him. We thought He would wear royal robes, but look at Him now, hanging half-naked and dying a shameful death on a cross." They thought His movement was over, crucified with Him. Matthew may have been considering going back to his tax tables, Peter back to his fishing. The disciples were sad and depressed and scared, but certainly much wiser. Later on, the disciples huddled in the Upper Room, fearing for their own lives. "After all," they reasoned, "if Jesus was crucified, dying a horrible death, it could also happen to us."

However, just forty days later, you would have heard their voices throughout the whole land, shouting with excitement and joy: "We've seen a dead man walking! We've been with Him and touched Him. He's alive! He's alive!" What changed them if it wasn't an empty tomb and a tangible experience of the risen Lord?

Second, if Jesus remained dead, how can you explain the faithfulness of the disciples to their testimony of the resurrection, even in the face of their own deaths? I have, in my time, told some lies, many of those whoppers. But when I'm caught, I immediately tell the truth, under the general theory that it's better to tell the truth and get out of it right away than to keep telling lies. If anyone ever put a gun to my head and said, "I'm going to pull the trigger unless you tell the truth," I would change my story without hesitating, even if I had been telling the truth already!

Something happened to the disciples. Peter was crucified upside down on a cross because he didn't want to die the way Jesus had. Peter could have easily gotten out of death had he said, "Look, I made it up. It didn't really happen." The reason he didn't say that was because he really did see a dead man walking. Peter wasn't the only one who died testifying to this reality. James was run through with a sword; Bartholomew was hacked to pieces; Paul had his head chopped off outside the walls of Rome; Stephen was stoned to death. Of the original twelve disciples, only one died of old age, and he was exiled to Patmos, a horrible island, cut off from almost everyone. Each of these men could have grown old in the wisdom and honor of days and patted the heads of their grandchildren. Not one did. They died as martyrs with the story on their lips that they had been with the risen Jesus, the One who had died, was buried, then left His grave immortal and glorified. Unless the disciples were telling the truth, they were fools.

Third, if Jesus remained dead, why did more than five hundred people say they saw Him alive? Take a look at 1 Corinthians 15:6. In excess of five hundred people said they saw Jesus after He died. Think about it. If just one person came to us and said he or she had seen a dead man walking, we would call the men in white jackets to come and handle the problem. If five came together and made the same claim, we might think it was a joke and just laugh it off. If ten got together and made such a claim, we would likely think it was a conspiracy. But more than five hundred people? We'd be crazy to ignore them. We'd at least go down and check the coffin. That's what happened when witness after witness claimed to have seen Jesus alive. People checked out their claims, and believed.

Fourth, if Jesus remained dead, how can you explain the credibility of the witnesses? We're so sophisticated. We think we're the only ones in the world to ask a question, to ever wonder about a dead man getting up from the grave. Think about it. In the first century, people questioned just as much as we do, but they had an advantage. They could go and ask the witnesses. And they did. And time after time, the witnesses' stories checked out. So what happened? Just what you'd expect. The Christian faith grew, in spite of intense persecution, to become the greatest religion in the history of the world.

Fifth, if Jesus remained dead, how can you explain the inability of the first century skeptics to provide a viable alternative explanation? All the power of Rome and of the religious establishment in Jerusalem was geared to stop the Christian faith. They had the perfect weapon. All they had to do was go to Jesus' grave site and produce His body for all to see. No one did. Why? There wasn't a corpse to produce. That corpse had gotten up, demonstrated His resurrection to hundreds of people over a forty-day period, then ascended into heaven and began ruling at the right hand of God the Father. So all the antagonists could do was try to kill off Jesus' followers, but they multiplied so fast the authorities couldn't keep up.

Sixth, if Jesus remained dead, how can you explain the reality of the Christian church and its phenomenal growth in the first three centuries of the Christian era? Christ's church had spread from Jerusalem and had covered the Western world by the fourth century. Do you seriously think a religious movement built on a lie could spread so quickly and often under the threat of the ultimate reprisal—death? The church didn't grow simply because it promoted love, peace, and happiness; it grew because a dead man left His grave alive.

If, after dealing with that kind of evidence, you still can't grant the possibility of the resurrection of Christ, you are simply not paying attention. You are also not considering the practical cost. Jesus rose from the dead—that's *fact*. But it's also *fact* that His resurrection guarantees the possibility of our being forgiven, of our experiencing power to live a grace-filled life, of our really finding meaning in life, of our holding on to the genuine hope of living forever beyond the grave.

The resurrection of Christ: fact or fiction? You decide.

TIME TO DRAW AWAY
❖

Read Luke 24, 1 Corinthians 15.

For meditation:

Do you ever doubt whether Jesus rose from the dead?
Do you ever question if Christianity is true or not? The
truth of Christianity stands or falls on the reality of Jesus'
resurrection. Review the evidence. Consider it
carefully. You may even want to read some other books
on the matter, such as Who Moved the Stone? *by Frank*
Morison or Knowing the Truth About the Resurrection
by William L. Craig. But remember,
whenever doubts about Christianity arise
in your mind, know that you can rest in the fact
of Christ's resurrection. The evidence is conclusive.

Born to Hope

T here are many objections to hope. As Christians, we've all heard the comments: "Your religion is just pie in the sky. Give me something I can see and feel and touch, something in the here and now, not some intangible in the by and by." Or, "The trouble with the Christian faith is that it's so heavenly minded that it's no earthly good."

The Christian faith is certainly built on hope, but is it really a pie-in-the-sky kind of hope? Does it have any basis in reality? And if so, can it help us make it through life in the here and now? I believe with my whole being that our Christian hope is as solid as the rock on which it's grounded—the resurrected Lord of all. He is our hope, our treasure. And it's not foolishness for a man to dig for buried treasure, is it? If a man digs and finds, then he is above all men wise and prudent. Our hope in Jesus is like that. He is our treasure, our great reward. And as we search for Him, as we stay heavenly minded, He will make us of earthly good. He will make our present, not just our future, meaningful and purposeful.

In 1 Peter 1:3-9, the Apostle Peter gives us ground upon which to stand. As Christians, we're born to a living hope. Peter says, in essence, "Look, your hope is alive because Jesus is alive. He rose from the dead. I was there. I saw the empty tomb, the risen Lord. I know. I touched Him, I ate with Him, and I walked with Him at that breakfast by the Sea of Galilee." It's true. The soft sound of sandaled feet is as real today as it was in the first century. You and I were born to a living hope.

What does *hope* mean? The outcome of our hope is this—safety, soundness, for the rest of our lives. Peter gives us five promises of hope. Let's check them out.

Promise one: *Our hope is imperishable.* "An inheritance that can never perish, spoil or fade—kept in heaven for you" (verses 3-4). That is some kind of guarantee! But not everyone has it.

I have a dentist friend who, during WW II when meat was scarce, was able to get a great amount of frozen meat. My friend commuted between cities, so he bought a suitcase and put all of this frozen meat in it and headed for home on the train. When he deboarded, he forgot his meat-filled suitcase. By the time he checked with the authorities and they found the suitcase, seven long days had passed. My friend said, "By then I didn't even want the suitcase, and the authorities didn't want it either."

A lot of people are selling their souls for that kind of price, the kind that will perish like forgotten meat. Scripture teaches, "Do not store up for yourselves treasures on earth, where moth and rust destroy, and where thieves break in and steal. But store up for yourselves treasures in heaven, where moth and rust do not destroy, and where thieves do not break in and steal. For where your treasure is, there your heart will be also" (Matthew 6:19-21). Our heavenly hope is imperishable.

Promise two: *Our hope and our lives are guarded by God Almighty.* "Who through faith are shielded by God's power until the coming of the salvation that is ready to be revealed in the last time" (1 Peter 1:5).

Anna and I don't really need to lock our doors at night, even though we do. Why? Because we have our German shepherd, Quincy, the wonder dog, to protect us. Quincy is bigger than any thief who might be interested in stopping by. However, when we do lock our doors, it's to protect the thieves, not us. Quincy will watch over us. But thieves? Well, they'd better not risk messing with Quincy. What's the point? Our eternal security depends on the size of our guard. And when that guard is the Lord of the universe, who needs to worry?

That's why I believe in the doctrine of the perseverance of the saints, the once-saved-always-saved idea. First Peter 1:5 tells me that the assurance of my destiny doesn't depend on me. My guard is God. He holds me in the palm of His hand. He protects me against those who would want to steal me away. And what thief could ever prevail against the all-powerful God?

Promise three: *The hope we have by faith leads to joy.* "In this you greatly rejoice" (verse 6). Jesus provides the commentary: "I have told you this so that my joy may be in you and that your joy may be complete" (John 15:11). And in talking about His crucifixion, He said, "I tell you the truth, you will weep and mourn while the world rejoices. You will grieve, but your grief will turn to joy. . . . Now is your time of grief, but I will see you again and you will rejoice, and no one will take away your joy" (John 16:20-22).

Promise four: *Our hope will be tested and will be proved sound.* "In this you greatly rejoice, though now for a little while you may have had to suffer grief in all kinds of trials. These have come so that your faith—of greater worth than gold, which perishes even though refined by fire—may be proved genuine and may result in praise, glory and honor when Jesus Christ is revealed" (1 Peter 1:6-7). That's a whole new slant on temptation.

I'm sometimes appalled by the view we have of God. I remember the days when I used to say to God, "Now Lord, don't make me suffer. Don't give me tests, because You already know what's in my heart. You already know where I stand, and I don't like this game. Let's play another." I rebelled at the idea that God would test me to find out where I stood. Peter tells us the truth. God tests us not for His benefit but for ours. God doesn't test you to find out how you're doing; He already knows that. He tests you so *you* might know. And once tested, assuming your faith is authentic, your faith will prove sound.

Promise five: *God has and will give us belief so that the belief itself will become a token of our genuine faith.* Check out 1 Peter 1:8: "Though you have not seen him, you love him; and even though you do not see him now, you believe in him and are filled with an inexpressible and glorious joy." Let me try to explain what Peter's saying here.

Fulton Ousler says that one of the greatest arguments against the Christian faith is the argument from the problem of pain: How could a good God allow or cause so much pain, hurt, and suffering in the world? He couldn't, therefore God either is not good or is nonexistent. Ousler relates how every time he heard that argument and felt terrible about his faith, he thought, *You know, that very argument shows me the reality of that which I hold.* Ousler said, "We look around the world and we see all of this suffering, pain, and hardship, and then wonder where in the world did we ever get the idea that there was a God of love? Some malicious fiend, maybe, or a prime mover who went away on vacation once he started it all, but a God of love? No way!" So then Ousler thought, *Where did we get the idea of a God of love in a world like this?* He came to this conclusion: "The way we got it was because it is really true. There is a God of love." The Apostle Peter is essentially saying the same thing.

If you believe, you believe against the odds. When you hold on to hope, you're hoping when most people don't see any reason for hope.

The very fact you believe the unbelievable and hope in the unhopeable means it's real. It's fact. But we have firm reason to hope: We have a risen Lord who proved Himself to be alive over and over and over again. The One who conquered death is our great hope, and He has secured for us a great future. What other reasons do we need? If you're a Christian, you're blessed beyond your greatest dreams. Your hope will be realized. And so will mine. All praise be to God!

TIME TO DRAW AWAY
———— ❖ ————
Read Psalm 42, Romans 8:18-39.

For meditation:

Although our hope is grounded in fact
(the fact of Jesus' resurrection),
its focus is set heavenward on God. Turn your thoughts
toward Him. Today, keep Him ever before you.
As an aid, you may want to write down one of the passages
listed above and carry it with you,
or put it up someplace where you will see it often.
The idea is to become more heavenly minded so you will
become of more earthly good. I like the way C. S. Lewis
put it in Mere Christianity: *"If you read history you will*
find that the Christians who did most for the present world
were just those who thought most of the next. . . .
Aim at Heaven and you will get earth 'thrown in':
aim at earth and you will get neither."

When God Got Specific

During his long trek to faith, the eighteenth-century founder of Methodism, John Wesley, asked his counselor, Zinzendorph, a lot of questions. One time Zinzendorph asked Wesley a question: "Mr. Wesley, do you believe that Christ died for your sins?"

Wesley answered, "I believe that Christ died for the sins of the world."

"But, Mr. Wesley," Zinzendorph said, "I didn't ask you that. Did Christ die for *your* sins?"

A good question.

In Matthew 16, you will remember Jesus went to His disciples, asking them, "Who do people say the Son of Man is?" (verse 13).

"Well," the disciples answered, "some say you are this and some say you are that."

After they told Him what others had said, Jesus asked, "But what about you? . . . Who do you say I am?" (verse 15).

That was a good question too.

At Christmas, God doesn't allow us to be general about who He is or what He's done for us. He gets specific. That's what Christmas is all about—when the God of the universe, the God no one knew for sure, loved and cared for us so much that He entered time and space in His Son: "The angel said to them, 'Do not be afraid. I bring you good news of great joy that will be for all the people. Today in the town of David a Savior has been born to you; he is Christ the Lord'" (Luke 2:10-11).

I have a friend who's a pastor. He told me one time that when he looked out over his congregation, "I get the feeling sometimes, as they sit there staring at me, that someone is about ready to stand up and make a motion, 'I move that we receive the information and be dismissed.'" One of the dangers of being a Christian, especially for a long time, is that of simply receiving the information, then being dismissed.

"This will be a sign to you . . ." (verse 12).

"I move we receive the information and be dismissed."

"The Word became flesh . . ." (John 1:14).

"I move we receive the information and be dismissed."

The baby in a manger, born to die on a cross for His people. . . .

"I move we receive the information and be dismissed."

God is specific with His people at Christmas, and that should change our lives.

For example, at Christmas God got specific about His *love*.

A Parisian painter in 1875 named Marcel de le Clure wrote a love letter to his beloved. Though that doesn't seem so strange, it is. In this love letter, he repeated three words 1,800,000 times: "I Love You." No one knows how she responded, but I have a guess.

What would you do differently if you knew God loved you? Most of us think of God as someone to be feared. There's some good in that: God *is* big and scary. But what would you do if you knew, really knew, that He loved you—no ifs, ands, or buts?

Second, in the incarnation, God got specific about His *choice*. I'm not going to get into all the ins and outs of the doctrine of election, but if you're a believer, the doctrine of election teaches that, from the foundation of the earth, God knew your name. How would you act if you knew that before you were ever born, He planned everything you're going through right now? Would it give you a sense of comfort or relief? How would you act if you knew that before He hung the stars, before He hollowed out the valleys and created the mountains, that He called you to Himself, knew your name, planned your life, and fixed it so that you would know Him? I don't know about you, but that makes a big difference to me.

He came for His own; He entered time and space. And if you were the only person on the face of the earth, believer, He would have come for you.

Third, at Christmas, God got specific about His *promise*.

Cyprian, who was Bishop of the church at Carthage in the third century, once wrote to his young friend, Donatus:

This is a cheerful world as I see it from my garden under
the shadows of my vines. But if I were to ascend some high
mountain and look out over the wide lands, you know very well
what I should see: brigands on the highways, pirates on the
sea, armies fighting, cities burning. In the amphitheaters men

murdered to please applauding crowds; selfishness and cruelty and misery and despair under all roofs. It is a bad world, Donatus. . . . It is an incredibly bad world.

It really is a bad world. We need some light; we need some promise. That's what Christmas is all about.

It's hard to have faith in this kind of world. It's hard, but He's come and He's promised.

If you knew all of this was going to work out, every bit of it; if you knew you were going to get home safely; if you knew that nothing would happen to you this year that hadn't first passed through a nail-scarred hand; how would you act?

Fourth, God was also specific about *our response.*

Clovis Chappell tells the story about one of the shepherds who heard the proclamation of the angels about the birth of Jesus but did not go to Bethlehem to see for himself. Decades later, as he held his grandson on his knee, he told the child the stirring story about Jesus and the angels.

"Is that all?" asked the boy. "What did you do when you heard the good news? Was it true? Was the Christ child really born?"

The old man replied, with some sadness, "I never knew. Some say it was true; some say it was only a dream. I didn't take the trouble to go and see."

Christmas didn't just happen two thousand years ago. It happened in us, if we have seen Him and believed.

Have *you?* If not, don't wait any longer. Go and see. Go and see Him for yourself. Don't pass up the opportunity anymore.

If, on the other hand, you have seen Jesus and believed, let Christmas be celebrated through you, not just one time a year, but all year long, every year. It's not just about a baby, you know. It's about Christ the Lord, the living God, coming to see you and me, coming to live and die for us. That should make all the difference, all the difference in the world.

TIME TO DRAW AWAY
———— ❖ ————
Read Isaiah 9:6-7, Luke 2:1-20.

For meditation:

Do you really know God's love? Can you truly rest in His choice? Have you trusted in His promise? Even if you can answer yes to these questions, there are still depths to be explored in these matters that will deepen your relationship with the Lord. So ponder each question and the issues each raises. If need be, review this chapter so you can better reflect on these things. How should you respond to Him in light of these truths? What differences should they make in your life right now, today? Seek the Lord's enabling strength to initiate change.

Those Annoying Interruptions

Have you ever noticed how annoying interruptions in a busy schedule are often divine appointments? That happens to me a lot, but I hardly ever remember that when I'm interrupted. Let me tell you what happened just this morning.

I got a call from a young man who insisted that he talk to me. I was up to my ears in work. I had just returned from a week working out of town, and I was preparing material for an upcoming speaking engagement. I had spent the day before teaching (hours of lectures) at the seminary. I had a pile of letters to answer, and I had to compose an update letter for those on the radio ministry's mailing list. And . . . well, I just felt somebody else could deal with this man's problem. To be honest with you, I was also quite irritated that I was being asked to drop everything I was doing to deal with something I felt could be handled by other staff members.

But God, with His strange sense of humor, arranged it so no one else was around to handle the call. I was sitting at the desk where the "buck stopped," so I reached for the phone thinking, "Lord, I could do Your work better if it weren't for all these people." Just before I started speaking to the young man, I thought I heard God say, "Child, these people *are* your work."

As I soon discovered, this young man was in Florida for the day. Before he went back to California (his home), he wanted to talk to me about the emptiness he felt only six months after becoming a Christian. I listened as he told me his story.

"When I first became a Christian, all I could think about was how wonderful it was that Jesus loved me. I told others about it; I prayed a whole lot; I was happy being with my new family. And then something happened. I didn't feel His presence anymore. Then I started doing some of the things I did before I became a Christian. I started thinking that if I really knew Christ, I wouldn't have the kind of thoughts I have and I wouldn't do the things I do."

He then told me what he had felt and known the moment he received Christ. He told me about the terrible conviction of sin and the tremendous relief when he discovered the grace of God through the sacrifice of Christ.

"But," he said, "that was then and this is now. I'm not sure anymore about anything. I am plagued with doubts and I am so afraid. There is this emptiness and loneliness that I feel almost all the time."

Then he asked the question he had called to ask: "Dr. Brown, do you think I'm really a Christian? Do you think I'm not saved? And if I'm not, what can I do to be saved?"

I told him about the devil and how Jesus called Satan "the accuser." I told him that all the condemnation he was receiving didn't come from God. I told him about the assurance of salvation and how one obtained it. I told him that the very fact he was talking to me showed to whom he really belonged. If he did not belong to Christ, I told him, he certainly would not have called me. He simply would have walked away from God's people in silence. I told him that if he wasn't a Christian, God had lied to him, and if God had lied, we had a bigger problem than whether or not he was saved.

And then I thought (I suspect it was from the Father) about the parable of the prodigal son (Luke 15:11-32). I related the story to the young man. I reminded him that the son who was living with the pigs was no less the son of his father while with the pigs than when he was home with the father. He had just run away from home. That was all.

Then I said to the young man: "You are going back home to California this afternoon and that is an important home. But there is another home Jesus was talking about in the parable. It is the home we find when we go to our heavenly Father. Go home to California this afternoon, but, son, go back to your other home, the one where the Father always waits."

I reminded him that home was where the love was. I told him that it wasn't important that he be perfect, only home.

He was helped, I think. He was laughing before he hung up the phone, and it was the laughter of the redeemed. I was glad I could help, but, after all, I had a lot of work to do and was relieved to be able to get back to it.

That was when the Lord spoke again: "That call was for you, you know."

"What do you mean, it was for me?" I replied. "I helped one of Your children who was in trouble and needed a brother."

"You're one of My children too."

"I already knew that. I don't need assurance of salvation."

"I know you don't. But you do need to go home sometimes too because that *is* where the love is. That is where I am."

Then I remembered my quick prayers, my heavy schedule, and the "important ministry" in which I'm involved. I hadn't stopped long enough to sense that I was lonely, just like the young man to whom I had spoken. In the stillness, I realized that I felt empty too.

You can cover that for a while if you are busy enough. You can pretend that you aren't lonely if you are with enough people enough of the time. You can hide the emptiness that can be healed only with the Father's love at home if you can keep saying spiritual things and talking God-talk.

I felt guilty when I thought about the waiting Father at home. The guilt didn't come from my sin (though, God knows, there is plenty of that) but from the fact that I had not gone to Him. I had been too busy to go home where the love was.

And so, the rest of the morning and a considerable part of the afternoon, I repented. I, as the son in the parable, "came to myself" and remembered my home and my Father.

I was kind of worried when I thought about Him and home. Would my Father be angry? Would He reject me? Would He cast me out? That is, of course, what I deserve. But He didn't do that. He didn't even let me finish my apology. He met me on the way and He wasn't angry—He was laughing! How about that? He was laughing.

His words were similar to the ones heard so long ago in the story told by Jesus. He said that He had missed me and the time we spent together. He assured me of my place at home and, as silly as it sounds, at home with the Father we had a party.

Perhaps you have been away from home lately. Perhaps you were busy about the Father's business and just didn't have time to spend with Him. Perhaps you were worried that He wouldn't forgive you or accept you. Maybe you wondered if He even remembered you because it's been so long. It could be that you were afraid that He wouldn't be there.

I have some good news. He's there. I checked. You go on home because home is where the love is.

TIME TO DRAW AWAY
— ❖ —
Read Zephaniah 3:17, Luke 15:11-32.

For meditation:

Like the earthly father who gleefully welcomed his wayward son home, so our heavenly Father delights in us when we return to our home with Him. If you've been gone for awhile, don't stay away. Whatever has come between you and your Father can be overcome. Go back home. Talk to Him. Let Him speak to you. He loves you more than you could ever imagine. Allow Him to show you once again.

The Coming of the King

Sometime ago, a friend gave me an article from *Working Mother* magazine called "Barbie and the Three Wise Men." In this article, the author Kim Wiley told about a beautiful and expensive crèche she had bought to give her children so they could learn some of the values she had received from her parents. After explaining to her kids the significance of the manger scene, she was startled the next morning to see a nude Barbie doll and a headless Ken doll standing in the crèche. As she reached into the manger scene to remove the dolls, she heard her little girl's challenge: "But Mommy, they brought gifts to the baby Jesus too." So Mrs. Wiley left Barbie and Ken in the crèche.

Over the next few days, a variety of dolls, cuddly bears, and other stuffed animals found their place before the manger and the Christ child. Her children had not responded as she had intended, but she admitted that they had clearly understood the message of the crèche.

One of the difficult things for a Christian to do at Christmas is to focus. We know, of course, that Christmas is the birthday of the King, but in our day it has become a whole lot more than that. It has to do with family, with loving, with caring, with joy and celebration. As Christians, we are not against any of these things—indeed, they have their very foundation in the faith. But at times they lead us away from the center of Christmas.

And yet, even when we view Christmas through the lens of our Christian faith, we still often have trouble focusing. Does Christmas really have to do with angels? Are shepherds necessary ingredients to the whole story? What about the manger and the innkeeper? How much of it really reflects the reality of what we celebrate today as the birthday of the King? Perhaps, in order to focus, we need to get away from the traditional Christmas images without abandoning the reality behind those images. Let's try by taking a forward look from a backward perspective.

Isaiah the prophet lived 740 years before the birth of Christ, during

49

a time of great upheaval and persecution against the people of God. He was called to speak a word of hope when there wasn't any hope. Isaiah looked forward to a time of genuine assurance and exuberant joy that would accompany the coming of the Messiah. In Isaiah 9:6-7, a small section from the book Isaiah penned under the Spirit's guidance, we find a picture of this Messiah, the One who had not yet come. Perhaps taking a look at it will enhance our vision—we who are privileged to look back on the event Isaiah could only hope to one day discover.

First, note the gift of the King: "For to us a child is born, to us a son is given" (verse 6). Whose Son? The Son of God, the One who came, suffered, and died for us. In that wonderful gift, we can see a magnificent sacrifice.

During WWII, a bereft father lost his son. In his time of tremendous grief, the father was comforted by his pastor. But as often happens when someone hurts so deeply, he said some things he didn't mean. This father was angry over what had happened to his son and angry with God that He had let his son die. The nearest person he could find to God was his pastor, so he let him have it.

"Where was your God when my son was killed?" he shouted at the pastor as tears rolled down his cheeks.

With understanding and compassion, the pastor quietly answered: "In the same place He was when His own Son was killed."

The Father's gift of His Son is His way of saying to us that our lives have meaning and He cares deeply about what we're going through. It's not simply about a nice baby in a manger, or about shepherds, singing, and celebration—all of which may give us some good feelings. That's not enough. Our problems are too deep for platitudes and warm fuzzies. If there is a God, He must speak to us in a way that really makes a difference. And He has. He gave us His Son, even to the point of leading Him to the cross to give up His life for us.

Second, notice the government of the King: "The government will be on his shoulders" (verse 6). Jesus didn't come just to help a few people, to say some nice things about peace, joy, and love, and to give us a warm feeling in the middle of a cold night. Jesus came to establish the Kingdom, to inaugurate a government, to announce the control of the God of the universe.

On the night of Lincoln's death, a crowd of fifty thousand people gathered in front of the Exchange Building in New York City. Emotions were running high, and people were worried. In fact, there was a good chance that the crowd would become a mob and violence would erupt. Then a man in an officer's uniform stepped out on the building's balcony. His voice, clear and sharp, cut through the babble of the crowd: "Fellow citizens! Clouds and darkness are round about Him. His pavilion is dark waters, and thick clouds of the skies. Justice and judgment are the establishment of His throne. Mercy and truth go before His face. Fellow citizens, God reigns and the government in Washington still lives." Instantly, the crowd was stilled. That man's name was James A. Garfield. Years later, he became President of the United States, and he, too, was assassinated.

In an earlier time of human turmoil, God entered time and space through His Son. He stood in the midst of the confused, angry, fearful crowd and announced that the King had come to proclaim the arrival of His Kingdom. He said it was a Kingdom that would not fail because it had a King nobody elected and nobody could dethrone. For a time, the crowd followed Him and praised Him too. But later they turned on Him and killed Him. Was the Kingdom now dead? Not in the least! It carried on, it spread, it gained more and more support, and one day, He will return to smash His enemies and solidify His rule for all eternity. Christ is already in Christmas for the citizens of the Kingdom, and He will be in everyone's Christmas, but in some quarters, His rule will not be cause for celebration.

Third, note from Isaiah's perspective the grandeur of the King: "He will be called Wonderful Counselor, Mighty God, Everlasting Father, Prince of Peace" (verse 6). What's in a name? The essence of that which is named. And the essence of the King is strength, benevolence, eternity, joy, wisdom, shalom.

Only fools question the existence of the King. The core issue has always been, What is He like? not, Does He exist? Christmas is when God revealed His very nature, His very essence, in His Son, Jesus Christ.

How much we misread the God of the universe. Did you ever think that the manger is a hug from a God we thought was a policeman? Did you ever think that the little baby was the soft whisper of a God who didn't want to frighten the people He loved? Did you ever think that the pastoral scene was God appearing in human form so He wouldn't turn the very people away whom He wanted to draw to Himself? How great is the grandeur and grace of the King!

Fourth, Isaiah also looked forward to the growth of the Kingdom: "Of the increase of his government and peace there will be no end. He will reign . . . over his kingdom, establishing and upholding it with justice and righteousness from that time on and forever. The zeal of the Lord Almighty will accomplish this" (verse 7). I have an announcement to make: The Kingdom has come and the Kingdom is coming. You can't stop it. Neither can anyone else.

Two women walked by a department store and saw in the window a crèche with shepherds, angels, Mary, Joseph, and the baby Jesus. "How about that?" said one of the ladies. "The church is trying to horn in on Christmas too."

Lady, you don't understand. The King owns Christmas. He owns the department store. Even if you don't know it, He owns you. And furthermore, you can't stop Him.

Christmas isn't only a time when Christians remember the first coming of the King. It's a time when we look forward to His Second Coming. The first time He came as a baby; the second time He will come with His mighty legions. The first time you can receive Him the easy way; the second time you will accept Him the hard way. December 25th is the time to meet Jesus in a manger. But we dare not forget that the baby has grown up. He is now the King of kings, and one day He'll return in earth-shaking power, toppling His enemies and rewarding His friends and reclaiming what is rightfully His.

Are you ready to face Him?

TIME TO DRAW AWAY
❖

Read Isaiah 65–66, Revelation 20–22.

For meditation:

*If you're a child of the King, whether Christmas is close
at hand or not, why don't you throw a party? That's
right—put aside some time to celebrate the King's birthday.
Send out invitations, prepare the goodies, get some party
decorations, plan some games . . . have a ball! One day*

*we'll be able to celebrate forever, so why not get a head
start and begin enjoying Him more now?*

*If, however, you're struggling with the King's rule or you're
not sure about your relationship with Him, He invites you
into His throne room to talk to Him about anything that's
on your mind or heart. He always has time for you,
so take advantage of His mercy and grace. Go.
Set things straight. Then plan a party!*

How to Believe

If you were ever a skeptic, you probably experienced going to a Christian to ask questions only to hear that person say, "Well, you just have to believe. That's all, just believe." I had the same experience. And I don't know about you, but even though I knew the advice was sincere, I felt it deserved to be rated on a scale with the person who sees me shaking before boarding an airplane and says, "Now, Steve, don't be afraid. Just believe that everything will be okay." In both cases, I already know the problem. What I need is a solution, and this advice doesn't provide one.

Jesus said a lot of amazing things about belief. He said with belief in Him we could move mountains because with Him nothing was impossible. James added that we could have wisdom if only we believed. That's all fine and it's the truth, but how do I believe? How do I move beyond doubt to trust? If belief is the answer, how do I obtain it? We can find some answers to these questions in the story of the official's son found in John 4:46-54.

When we read this text, one of the first things we learn is that belief is born out of need. In John 4, the official's son was sick and dying. Out of sheer panic and fear, the man begged Jesus to heal his son (verses 46-47). Here was a man in desperate need, and it was because of his desperation that he was ready to trust in Jesus' ability to heal his son. If you have no need to believe, you will not believe.

A lot of Christians say they believe in the perseverance of the saints, meaning eternal security, the doctrine that once we're saved we're always saved. Yet, when you look closer you discover that they don't really believe that. I said I believed in eternal security for a long time, until one night I realized how bad I really was, how little I deserved, and I panicked. It was out of that need that I really learned to believe. It's a paradox, but the difference between strong faith and weak faith is need. The strongest Christian really is the Christian who knows how weak he or she is.

God is in the business of putting His children in holes so deep that they can't possibly get out without His help. What is your need right now? Whatever it is, rejoice. That's God's hole, and while you're in it, He's going to teach you how to believe.

John 4 also teaches us that belief is nurtured in Christ. Whether or not your belief grows depends on the object of that belief. And if it's anchored in the wrong object, belief will sink and drown. So when you're in a hole, make sure you reach out to Christ. Are you hurting? In doubt? Struggling? Go to Him. That's how your belief will be nurtured.

John 14:12 teaches that "anyone who believes in himself will do what Jesus did." No, that's not what it says. It says, "Anyone who believes in the power of positive thinking will do what Jesus did." Wrong again. Does it say, "He who believes in the power of the church will do what Jesus did"? Not at all. It does say, however, that "anyone who has faith in me will do what I have been doing. He will do even greater things than these, because I am going to the Father." I know it's almost a truism, but it's one a lot of Christians miss: Belief will not grow unless the object of that belief is Jesus Christ.

Another truth about belief is that it's grown only in faith. Jesus healed the official's son, and the man responded in faith. Then "Jesus replied, 'You may go. Your son will live.' The man took Jesus at his word and departed" (John 4:50). The official accepted what Jesus said about reality even when he didn't yet know firsthand the reality for himself.

You say you believe. How much are you willing to bet on that belief? Your money, your life, your relationships, your friends? Without risk, there can be no belief. When Jesus told the man who had been sick for a number of years, "Pick up your mat and walk" (John 5:11), the man could have said, "Are you out of your mind? I can't walk." And he would have remained a cripple. When Peter and John were at the temple with the lame beggar calling out to them, Peter healed the beggar with "In the name of Jesus Christ of Nazareth, walk" (Acts 3:6). What if the beggar had said, "I don't believe you. Go away"? If he had done that, he would have stayed at the temple gate begging until the day he died.

Satan's syndrome is this: A believer says, "I believe and I am secure in my belief. But if I risk it, I might lose it; I might find that it isn't true. Therefore, I'm not going to risk it." Within the context of your faith, God is telling you to risk. Belief grows in proportion to faith, and another word for *faith* is *risk*.

The final lesson about belief from John 4 is this: Belief is matured in fact. Jesus was right. The mature believer is the one who has seen God act in direct and specific ways, whose faith cannot be shaken—ever—because it is built on fact.

How do you get to belief? You have a need; you risk; you invest your trust in the proper object; then the Father acts in ways that will simply leave you speechless. That's when you'll have that John 4 experience: "So he [the official] and all his household believed" (verse 53). That is the Father's surprise! Paul said it right, "Now to Him who is able to do immeasurably more than all we ask or imagine, according to his power that is at work within us" (Ephesians 3:20).

A mature Christian is not the one who says, "Lord, zap me with faith and belief so that I can do the mountain bit." The mature Christian is the one who has gone through the process of need, Christ-centered help, faith, and risk . . . and has seen God faithful.

The one sport I have ever excelled at is swimming. I have even taught many people to swim. If you are swimming in competition, I can show you how to cut time off your speed. Swimming is an experienced fact to me, but that maturity in swimming never came in shallow water. I'll never forget the day when I was very small and my father let go of me in water that was much deeper than I was tall. The realization that I was in deep water and swimming was an absolute thrill. That day I laughed and laughed. My father laughed with me.

In the area of faith, the heavenly Father laughs for the same reason. Have you heard Him chuckle lately?

TIME TO DRAW AWAY
———— ❖ ————

Read 2 Corinthians 12:2-10; James 1:2-4,12.

For meditation:

*In a society that praises strength, it's very hard
for us to boast of our weakness. And yet,
as paradoxical as it may sound, when it comes to faith,
we're at our strongest when we're at our weakest.*

Are you feeling vulnerable, weak, afraid to risk? Great! You're in the perfect place for God to work His best. Just keep believing in Him, relying on Him to do what you feel unable to handle. He'll come through. Trust Him.

Tracking the Devil

I want to introduce you to a personality so evil that most Christians can't even comprehend it. I want to introduce you to a being who, from our standpoint at least, seems as evil as God is good; as selfish as God is unselfish; and as hateful as God is loving. His name is Satan, and he cares about you in a distorted, destructive way. The Apostle Paul warns us about him in Ephesians 6:10-12. Let's take a close look at this text. In fact, take a moment to read it now before continuing.

This passage makes it clear that Paul believed in the reality and personality of evil. One of the finest strategic moves Satan has ever performed was to convince people that he doesn't exist. So let me tell you why I believe in Satan.

I believe in a personal, real devil because Jesus warned me about him. Almost all of the clearest teaching we have about this fallen angel comes from the lips of Jesus Himself. Jesus is quite specific about how real the incarnation of evil in Satan is, and He spends a good deal of time warning us of the dangers of this perverted being (see John 8:31-49; 12:31; Mark 4:13-15; Luke 22:1-6,31-34). He knew about Satan firsthand. That demon tried to sabotage Jesus' mission before it even got going (Luke 4:1-13), and of course, he kept trying to subvert Jesus throughout His ministry, but he failed every time. Jesus is not the only witness to the devil's reality; many of the other biblical writers speak about him too. But when our Master tells us something personally, we should hang on every syllable and heed every word, even when we don't like what we hear. The doctrine of Satan is one of those truths I'd rather forget but I dare not.

Another reason I believe in the reality of the devil is because he's being discovered by modern man. We're a sophisticated age enmeshed in science and technology. Right? And yet, if we're so sophisticated, why are thousands upon thousands of Americans involved in the occult? Evil is a present reality of which Christians had better be aware. It's a reality that poses a clear and present danger to the Body of Christ.

58

I know. I have experienced the reality and personality of evil in my own life. I have seen Satan walking down the streets of a city slum. I have seen him in a bottle resting on the stomach of a drunk and smiling as the crowds line up to watch an "adult" movie. I have seen Satan's writing in the words of a suicide note and a hate letter. I have seen Satan in the hurt, emptiness, and frustration of humanity. Sometimes, late at night when I can't sleep, I have seen Satan in the fear, anger, and guilt of my own life. Satan is real, and he's actively destroying lives.

Ephesians 6 also tells us that the devil "schemes" (verse 11). Satan doesn't come up and say, "Hi, I'm the devil, and I'm going to destroy you." He comes as a mysterious stranger, as one who cares, who understands, and who's willing to listen. Then he attacks, often subtly, but always viciously. The Bible calls Satan the tempter (Matthew 4:3, 1 Thessalonians 3:5) and the accuser (Revelation 12:10) and the father of lies (John 8:44). Satan accuses us before God, trying to tempt God to turn on us with his lies. Satan also lies to us, trying to tempt us to turn against God.

When you've had a mountaintop experience and then sinned, have you ever had the thought, "If you really are a Christian, you wouldn't do that"? You didn't get that from God. Satan likely planted that lie in your mind. Have you heard the slander that comes from Christians about other Christians? Have you heard the anger, the bitterness, and the lies that rail against the truths of God?

Someone has said that the devil tempts youth with beauty, the ambitious with power, and the rich with gold. Satan is crafty, and he's terribly good at what he does. He always says, "Take what you want and pay for it later." And believe me, when you take from Satan, he'll be sure you repay the debt.

In Ephesians 6 Paul also helps us see that the battle against evil in which we're engaged is not psychological, not financial, not administrative, not human. It is demonic, spiritual, supernatural. It transcends our world of taste, sight, sound, smell, and touch. And yet, it permeates our world and threatens us at every turn.

In seminary I learned a lot of things. I learned administration and pastoral counseling. I did my clinical work at a mental hospital. I learned theology, biblical studies, church history, and a slew of other wonderful things. But nobody taught me how to pray. Nobody taught me how to get on my knees and storm the gates of heaven against the power of the evil one. Take a look at the supernatural battle in Judges 7. Gideon goes out to fight with thirty-two thousand men against the even stronger forces of the Midianites. He knows his army is insufficient against the opposing army, nevertheless Gideon hears God tell him that his army is too large—he needs to do some trimming. So Gideon asks anybody who's afraid to fight to leave. Twenty-two thousand men walk out on him. Now, he has only ten thousand troops. So Gideon says, "All right, guys, I know we're outnumbered even more than before, but we'll go out and fight anyway."

God, however, had other plans. He told Gideon, "You still have too many men. I will help you reduce their number by the way they drink their water." What a way to pick an army! After the men had quenched their thirst, Gideon was left with only three hundred men. Now if I had been Gideon, I would have gotten out of there. There's no way three hundred men could possibly win a battle that thirty thousand men would have likely lost. And yet, at that point God told Gideon, "Get up, go down against the camp, because I am going to give it into your hands" (Judges 7:9). And Gideon obeyed, and God gave him victory. That's the battle supernatural.

Returning to Ephesians 6, the Apostle Paul tells us that as human, finite creatures, we have lost the supernatural battle, but as children of the King, we have already won it. How can that be? It's very simple: "The one [Christ] who is in you is greater than the one [Satan] who is in the world" (1 John 4:4). Many Christians believe Satan, not God, is sovereign. They look under their beds, behind their dressers . . . everywhere for demons, seeing the demonic in every facet of their lives. To them I offer a reminder: Satan does nothing except by the permission of God, the only true sovereign. God is in control of the supernatural battle, not the devil and his cohorts. And He has already won the war. James 4:7 states, "Resist the devil, and he will flee from you." Why is that? It's not because we're so smart or have the power. It's because he has been defeated by Christ at Calvary.

When I was growing up, a bully moved into my neighborhood. He was about four years older than I was, and one day he decided it was time to pick on me. This bully came into my front yard and scared me to death. After a few long, tense moments, I decided the only way I could get this guy to back off was to stand up against him, so I held my ground. Much to my surprise, he became scared. He started to tremble all over! I said to myself, *Man, I'm really something!* Then I heard a noise and turned around and noticed my father, standing behind me on the front porch. I hadn't terrified that bully, but the presence of my father sure had.

It's the same way for us as believers. Except our Father isn't standing behind us—He's active in us through the presence of His Son and the power of His Spirit. Who could ever challenge Him and win? No one, not even Satan and all the power of hell. The devil doesn't stand a chance.

TIME TO DRAW AWAY
———— ❖ ————

Read 1 Peter 5:8-11, Revelation 12.

For meditation:

How are you faring in this supernatural war?
Are you aware of what's going on around you? If not, ask
God to make you more sensitive to the spiritual conflict.
Do you find yourself struggling with how to wage
an effective campaign against the evil one? Meditate
on Ephesians 6:10-18. There you'll learn what armor
and weapons will best equip you for the fight.
Whatever your situation, please don't ignore or shrink
away from this battle. Either mistake will make you
easy prey for the enemy.

Remember, God has already won the war against Satan.
Now all that's left are some rebel pockets of resistance,
and that's where you and I come in. As long as we carry
on the fight in God's power and wisdom, wearing His armor
and using His weapons, we can't lose.

This Is Not an Abandoned World

While I was driving home the other day, I saw the ugliest car I have ever seen. This car wasn't just ugly—it was ugly on top of ugly. It had a large gash on its side; one of the doors was held together with baling wire; and several other body parts were almost completely rusted out. The car's muffler was so loose that with every bump, it hit the street, sending sparks in every direction. I couldn't tell the original color of the car. The rust had eaten away much of the paint, and so much of the car had been painted over with so many different colors that any one of them (or none of them) could have been the first coat. The most interesting thing about the car was the bumper sticker: "THIS IS NOT AN ABANDONED CAR."

We live in a fallen world, and sometimes it looks as ugly as that car. Almost everywhere you turn, you can see tragedy and heartache. Only a fool misses the point from the morning headlines that we are sitting on the edge of disaster.

But it isn't just the world. It's us. Sometimes the effort to keep on keeping on doesn't seem worth it. Guilt, loneliness, hurt, and fear become constant companions. One wonders sometimes if any of life makes any difference. One wonders about things such as home and meaning.

A long time ago, in a manger, a baby was born. He was a sign to us. His presence read, "THIS IS NOT AN ABANDONED WORLD."

During every Christmas season, there's a break in the bleakness; a bit of beauty in the middle of the ugliness shines through. People will laugh and make merry. Most won't understand why they laugh. Many of them will make merry because that is what one is supposed to do during the holiday season. But there are some who will pause and remember, "For unto us a child is born."

We have not been abandoned. Someday the Owner will return, then all the ugliness will be remedied. There won't be anymore pain, and all the tears will be dried.

May you live merrily because He came. Make your life merry because He keeps coming. Keep it merry because He is coming again to set all things right.

TIME TO DRAW AWAY

———— ❖ ————

Read Isaiah 11:1-9, Revelation 21:1–22:7.

For meditation:

Reflect on the passages just cited. Try to etch into your mind what the future holds for the children of the King. Then, as you face various hardships, recall your future with Him. And remember, just as He has prepared a great inheritance for His children, so has He chosen to prepare them to receive it. He is with you, even now, working in your life to make you ready for glory. You can find peace and joy in that.

Time to Do Something Different

Most January firsts are not that different than December thirty-firsts—just another date on the calendar. Sure, it's the beginning of a brand-new year and all of that, and people use it as a time to make various resolutions and enjoy fresh starts so they can lunge bravely into the future. But none of that ever made much sense to me. My job was the same, my family was the same, and my Father has always been the same yesterday, today, and forever. And so, to me at any rate, New Year's Day has always been just another day on the calendar. Until this last January first.

On that day my resignation as the senior pastor of the church I had served for seventeen years became effective. (No, they didn't fire me. That's not funny, you know.) And I became the professor of preaching at a nearby seminary and began devoting far more of my time to prayer, study, speaking, and writing. Sounds very spiritual, doesn't it? Well, it's not quite like that. Anna and I are also going to spend some time on the beach enjoying the fact that our children have become fine Christian young women who no longer need our constant oversight and parenting. We're going to take the time to "smell the flowers," and we're going to laugh a lot.

The point is this: This year is a time of major changes in our lives—and I hate change. I was perfectly content doing what I had always done. I was just walking down the road whistling a tune (a hymn, of course), and then God came and suggested that it was time to do something different. The King's suggestions are always commands, and when confronted with them, one either decides to run or do what He says. I've been walking with Him so long that I've forgotten how to run.

So here I am, having defined myself as a pastor for twenty-seven years, now a Christian broadcaster and a seminary professor. How about that sports fans? Sometimes I want to say with Saint Teresa, "Lord, You would have more friends if You treated the ones You had better." Of course, I wouldn't say that, and if I did, He would ask me where it was written that He was supposed to check with me anyway.

Aside from God, the only thing that never changes is the fact that there will always be change. Change is difficult. Lots of times when people I love move, friends or family go home to be with the Lord, I look in the mirror and find more signs of aging, or the Lord requires great change in me, I talk to Him about it. "Why," I ask Him, "does everything have to change? Why can't I just hold on to what I've got? I don't want a lot, Lord, and I don't ask for much except that what I've got stay the same."

Let me tell you what Anna said to me when I was going through the very difficult time of making a decision about resigning from the church. It wasn't the first time she had said it; in fact, she has said it to me a number of times. I asked her how she felt about it all, and she said, "Steve, I don't care where we go or what we do as long as I'm with you." That became my prayer to the Father: "Father, enable me to be with You as Anna has been with me. Enable me by Your grace to say, 'Lord, I don't care where we go or what we do as long as I'm with You.'" You see, He is our security and our home until we get home. The Scripture says, "For here we do not have an enduring city, but we are looking for the city that is to come" (Hebrews 13:14).

Our problem is that we keep trying to pretend that our transient city is a permanent one, and when the facts show us otherwise, we feel uncomfortable. We continue to claim promises that were meant for our final home as if they were given for our temporary abode. The fact is that we aren't home yet. The writer of Hebrews says it better than anybody: "All these people were still living by faith when they died. They did not receive the things promised; they only saw them and welcomed them from a distance" (Hebrews 11:13). Now that's a sad though realistic fact. (Give that verse to your friends who say the Bible is unrealistic and tell them to put it in their pipe and smoke it.) But there's more. Listen to the rest: "Instead, they were longing for a better country—a heavenly one. Therefore God is not ashamed to be called their God, for he has prepared a city for them" (verse 16).

So, we have begun another year. I suspect that your year will be (and likely has been) full of changes too. I also suspect that you don't like change much more than I do. When we get home, though, there won't be any more changes, and except for the presence of Jesus, that will be the best thing about Heaven. Until we get there, I'll pray for you, and you pray for me. Let's ask the Lord to remind us that until we get home, He will be our home. He asked me to remind you.

TIME TO DRAW AWAY
——————— ❖ ———————
Read Hebrews 11:1-40, 12:22-29.

For meditation:

What changes are you going through or anticipating that may be creating some anxiety in your life or in the lives of those around you? Take those matters before God and share your concerns with Him. As a loving, caring Father, He's ready to listen and help. He just wants you willing to accept whatever answer He gives.
Are you willing? If not, He'll even help you with that—so go ahead and talk to Him.

The Ways of God

The Bible, said John Calvin, is God's baby-talk—God using finite words to communicate something of His infinite nature. In the Scriptures, we receive the true record of the acts, words, and thoughts of God Himself. But who is this God? What is He like? The Gospel of Mark 1:1-15 gives us four pictures of God. Let's check them out.

The first portrait shows us that God's timing is always perfect. "After John was put in prison, Jesus went into Galilee, proclaiming the good news of God. 'The time has come,' he said" (Mark 1:14-15). Elsewhere we read, "There is a time for everything, and a season for every activity under heaven . . . I thought in my heart, 'God will bring to judgment both the righteous and the wicked, for there will be a time for every activity, a time for every deed' " (Ecclesiastes 3:1,17). "But when the time had fully come, God sent his Son" (Galatians 4:4).

God isn't waiting just for the fun of it. He's waiting because He has a time for every matter under heaven. That's true in your life too. Right now, God's timing is perfect. You may have a husband or a wife who isn't a Christian. You may be going through tough times. You're asking, "Why does God wait? Why is it taking Him so long? Why won't He help?" God is waiting simply because His timing is better than yours. Don't push it. Wait on Him. God's timing is perfect. When His time has come, it will be done. In Matthew 6:34, Jesus said, "Therefore do not worry about tomorrow, for tomorrow will worry about itself. Each day has enough trouble of its own." God is sovereign over not just what we do but the time in which we do it.

My father became a Christian three months before he died of cancer. I had prayed for my father for years and years; so had my mother. Time and time again, I had cried out to God, "Why so long? Are You going to let him die in his sins? Aren't You going to draw him to Yourself?" Then, a short time before my father died, in the most beautiful conversion experience I've ever seen, he received Christ. Do you know what happened as a result? My father almost converted a whole hospital! I wanted to go out, grab the nurses and doctors, and say, "Come, I want you to watch a Christian man die. I want you to see how this thing really works." It dawned on me then how perfect and right God's timing really is. You can trust God.

The second portrait reveals that God's preparation is always appropriate. "'I will send my messenger ahead of you, who will prepare your way'—'a voice of one calling in the desert, "Prepare the way for the Lord, make straight paths for him"'" (Mark 1:2-3). In John 16:12, Jesus said to His disciples, "I have much more to say to you, more than you can now bear." In other words, "You aren't prepared yet so I'm not going to tell you until you're ready."

I share your questions and concerns.

"What will I do if I find I have cancer?"

"What if I sit down with my checkbook next month and there isn't enough money to make the mortgage payment?"

"What if my kids turn away and never come back?"

"What if I lose my job?"

But remember that God will bring nothing into your life for which He has not already adequately prepared you.

A young man facing the death of his mother came to me not too long ago and said, "When my mom dies, I'm afraid I won't be able to stand it. I'm afraid I'll fall apart, and I can't afford to." What I said to Him I got from the Word: "Son, when you go to face the death of your mother, God will pay the fare. You'll find His presence. You'll find that as you make the journey, God will prepare you." The man told me later that God did just that—He didn't let him down. He will prepare you too, He promises.

Portrait number three shows yet another side of God: namely, His signs are always sufficient. "As Jesus was coming up out of the water, he saw heaven being torn open and the Spirit descending on him like a dove. And a voice came from heaven: 'You are my Son, whom I love; with you I am well pleased'" (Mark 1:10-11). Not everyone standing around heard these words. It was a sign to bolster John and Jesus.

That's true for the transfiguration experience as well. Jesus, when He went up on the Mount of Transfiguration, took with Him three of His closest disciples—Peter, James, and John. They saw the Lord gloriously transfigured before them and Moses and Elijah speaking to Him, but no one else saw this sign. Indeed, if you check out the resurrection experience in the New Testament, you'll also find that Jesus didn't go to Herod. He didn't go to Joe Pagan and Jane Cynic. He showed Himself to believers (Saul of Tarsus being the exception to the rule). This confirms what Luke 11:29 states: "This is a wicked generation. It asks for a miraculous sign, but none will be given it except the sign of Jonah."

God, in His graciousness and in His love for you as a believer, will provide sufficient signs for your life so that you might grow in grace, finding your life completed in Jesus Christ at the end. God gives us signs to draw us to Himself. Think about the believers you know who have told you about that amazing coincidence in their lives, that certain person who just happened to be at that place at that time to tell them about Jesus.

Not only does God give us signs to draw us to Himself, He also give us signs in order to bolster our faith as believers. God reaches down and lets us know that He is here. God's signs are sufficient because He loves you. I've gone to Him and said, "Father, if you'd just reach down and let me see a miracle, I'll be faithful." God has said, "Would you go away if I gave you no miracle?" "No, Father," I've answered, "I'm in too deep." God always reminds me at that point, "Then you're not in need yet."

The fourth portrait unveils the fact that God's ways are always consistent. In Isaiah 53 there's a prophecy; in Mark 1:9 you find a fulfillment. God kept His word.

In later verses we discover that Jesus was led out into the wilderness and tempted. Let that hit you. The Son of God was really tempted. He wasn't playacting. It wasn't a game. He was genuinely tempted to sin. As Hebrews 4:15 tells us, "For we do not have a high priest who is unable to sympathize with our weaknesses, but we have one who has been tempted in every way, just as we are—yet was without sin."

It was necessary for Christ to be tempted because without temptation there is no purity (at least that's true on the human level). Without purity God's demands for a perfect sacrifice could not be met. And Jesus met every one of them! Like the fulfilled prophecy mentioned above, Jesus' temptation and the reason for it say to me that God is a systematic theologian. He is consistent. His plan is well thought out, and

He won't fail to fulfill every part of it. So you can trust Him. If God loves you today, He will love you tomorrow. You can put your faith in Him.

A friend asked Martin Luther one time, "When everybody turns against you, where will you be?" Martin Luther replied, "Right where I am now, in the hands of almighty God."

Change is constant, but Jesus Christ is the same yesterday, today, and forever. Don't ever forget that.

TIME TO DRAW AWAY

Read Exodus 3:1-22, 4:1-17.

For meditation:

*Throughout history, the Lord has prepared His people
to tackle whatever He has set before them.
The examples are endless: Abraham, Moses, Joshua,
Gideon, Daniel, Jesus, the twelve apostles, and Paul,
to name a few. You are no exception. Whatever you're
dealing with now and whatever lies ahead, the Lord
is actively equipping you to handle it.*

*But perhaps you don't feel that way. Maybe you feel
overwhelmed, angry, bitter . . . grossly ill-equipped,
and you don't know what to do with those feelings.
Take them to God, lay them at His feet, and ask Him to
help you deal with them. Remember, He is your adequacy,
your strength. And He works best when we don't feel
up to the task. Our strength is in our weakness, because it
forces us to rely on Him rather than on ourselves.
And when our strength is found in Him,
nothing can keep us down for long.*

Street-Smart Christians

We're called to be street-smart Christians. Jesus said, "I am sending you out like sheep among wolves. Therefore be as shrewd as snakes and as innocent as doves" (Matthew 10:16). Jesus wants us to be the smartest, the sharpest, and the most street-smart people in the world. If we aren't, it's simply because we haven't been instructed or we haven't listened well enough.

So here's a lesson in becoming street smart. It comes from our master Teacher, Jesus. And it centers around a question with which the religious establishment (the Pharisees) and the political leaders (the Herodians) tried to trap Jesus. The question? "Is it right to pay taxes to Caesar or not?" (Matthew 22:17). If Jesus said yes, the Pharisees, who were looking out for Israel's interests, would denounce Him as disloyal to their country. If Jesus said no, the Herodians, who supported Roman rule, would denounce Him as a traitor to Rome and seek His execution. It seemed they had Him in a Catch-22 situation—no matter what He said, He was doomed. Or was He? This entire event gives us several lessons in evil, Satan, our fallen world, and how we can survive with the street-smarts of Jesus. Hear the lessons well.

The first lesson is this: *Evil's position is always uncomfortable.* Evil can't stand to be in the presence of good, and it certainly can't tolerate the persistence of good. It must do all it can to destroy the goodness around it. Why? Because goodness shames evil. It exposes evil for what it is, and by doing so it threatens evil's very existence. You see, the holiness of God tolerates only that which is holy, and that excludes evil. Holiness cannot keep company with evil, and even if it could, evil could not stand in the light of holiness. That's why Jesus was so disturbing to the Pharisees and the Herodians. And that's why Jesus is so disturbing to some of you.

Someone told me about two planes landing at the Jackson, Mississippi, airport. The tower had radioed to Delta flight 202 that they were cleared for landing on runway B. Then the controller told the

71

pilot of Eastern flight 467 that he was also cleared to land on runway B. The Delta pilot heard the transmission and radioed back to the tower: "Hey, wait a minute, you just told Delta flight 202 and Eastern flight 467 to land on the *same* runway." The tower was dead silent. Finally, the controller's voice came on the air: "Well, yeah, y'all be careful now."

That's what Christians are telling the world: "You're headed on a collision course of death and destruction. Jesus is the way, the truth, and the life, and there is no way to get to the Father except through Him. Don't land on any other runway. Evil will try to deceive you, but don't listen. If you do, you'll crash and burn."

The second lesson is equally important: *Evil's hatred is unified.* Look at Matthew 22:15-16. It shows that the Pharisees and the Herodians united in their attempt to trap Jesus. But these two groups couldn't have been further apart in their loyalties and ideologies. The Pharisees were the religiously orthodox of their day, and they felt that they should have nothing to do with Rome. The Herodians, on the other hand, were a political party, and they were committed to supporting Rome. These groups didn't communicate to each other, socialize, or do anything together. They despised each other, but they joined forces once—when they agreed to stop Jesus.

The world is hardly unified about anything, except in its hatred of us. Have you ever noticed that? So don't be surprised if you're singled out as a target because of your faith. A street-smart Christian knows that the forces of evil may hate each other, but they hate us and what we stand for even more.

The third lesson: *Evil's nature is underhanded.* I'm not big on conspiracy theories (you can find a conspiracy around every corner if you look hard enough and twist the facts well enough), but I do believe that evil is planned. Satan, with a lot of help from his friends, is a master planner.

Only a fool would miss the fact that, among other things, sexual mores in America have radically changed. What is surprising about that is just how fast they have changed. The sexual liberties (really enslavement) that would have shocked our culture only ten or fifteen years ago are accepted as normal today. Do you believe that's an accident?

A street-smart Christian knows that evil is planned. Drugs are not just something to do at a Saturday night party. Prostitution isn't just two consenting adults having a good time. Evil is organized and it's dangerous.

Fourth, Jesus teaches us that *evil's motive is ulterior*. Take a look at Matthew 22:16 and the way the leaders approached Jesus. They tried to take Him off guard with flattery. Flattery is the most dangerous arrow in the enemy's quiver.

A number of years ago a group approached me to do motivational speaking. They said that I was wonderful and the best speaker they had ever heard. Then they started talking about the great amount of money I would make if I would consent. If it wasn't for a friend of mine, Fred Smith, I probably would have fallen and accepted their offer. When I told him about the proposal, Fred said, "Steve, that's the dumbest thing I have ever heard. God called you to teach the Bible."

Christian businessperson, when they start telling you how wonderful you are, watch out, they're getting ready to con you; Christian single, when they start telling you how beautiful you are, it's a prelude to a pass; Christian student, when they start telling you how brilliant you are, watch for the kicker. Believe me, it will come. It's one of evil's best MO's.

Fifth, know that *evil's patience is undying*. Jesus gave an insightful answer to the question posed by the Pharisees and the Herodians. It was so good, in fact, that "when they heard [it], they were amazed. So they left him and went away" (verse 22). It seemed that Jesus had dealt a death-blow to the opposition. But He didn't. We see later on in Matthew that Judas, one of Jesus' closest followers, betrayed Him and set Him up for execution.

Have you ever seen those horror movies that seem to end with the monster's death? Just when you think the monster's down for good, he suddenly comes back to life and sets out to wreak havoc again. That is evil's way. The way of evil in the world and in our heart is that it, like the possum, frequently plays dead until we turn our back, then it rises up and gets us from behind. A street-smart Christian will remember that.

Finally, *evil's defeat is unconditional*. No matter how sneaky, how conniving, how resilient evil is, it will meet its match. Evil will go down for the final count and never raise its ugly head again. Our Lord made this quite clear: "Then he will say to those on his left, 'Depart from me, you who are cursed, into the eternal fire prepared for the devil and his angels'" (Matthew 25:41).

Paul Harvey shared a bumper sticker with his listeners: "Nature always bats last." That's not quite true. But it is true that God always bats last. That should never be forgotten. Evil has no existence on its own. Like a parasite, it can only survive by trying to suck the life blood out of goodness, light, and love. That is why atheists don't build hospitals except to make money. That is also why pagans don't send missionaries to feed the poor and clothe the naked. The very existence of evil depends on the existence of good, even ultimate Good.

Someday, however, God will discard evil forever. Just make sure before that happens that you haven't chosen the wrong side. A street-smart Christian knows the difference and has made the right choice.

TIME TO DRAW AWAY
——— ❖ ———
Read Proverbs 2, 2 Peter 2.

For meditation:

Are you aware of the evil influences in your life? Can you pinpoint something or someone who is trying to lead you away from what's true and right? Or have you already taken the bait and found yourself caught in evil's trap?

Take an honest inventory of your situation, beginning inwardly with your thoughts, then moving outward to your words, actions, and relationships. Invite the Holy One to help you identify and root out any of evil's inroads. The process may be painful at first, but the benefits will last for an eternity.

CHAPTER TWO

HURDLES WE FACE ABOUT OURSELVES

❖

*Now the proper good of a creature is
to surrender itself to its Creator—to enact
intellectually, volitionally, and emotionally,
that relationship which is given in the mere fact of its
being a creature. . . . In the world as we now know it,
the problem is how to recover this self-surrender.
We are not merely imperfect creatures who must
be improved: we are . . . rebels who must lay down
our arms. The first answer, then, to the question why
our cure should be painful, is that to render back
the will which we have so long claimed for our own,
is in itself, wherever and however it is done,
a grievous pain.*

C. S. Lewis
The Problem of Pain

Only Sinners Welcome

A while back I was talking to Doug Hall, one of my friends. He has a wonderful ministry in the inner city of Boston, and he's been serving there with great integrity and faithfulness for as long as I can remember. I asked him how things were going in Boston, and he told me they were in a very high growth mode. He talked about the great number of new churches that had been planted in the city and the explosive growth those churches had experienced, not from Christians transferring from other congregations, but from unbelievers finding Christ and joining these churches for the nurturing of their faith.

I have always admired Doug. He and his wife have stayed in the city at great personal cost, long after others left in frustration and disillusionment. I once asked Doug if he was going to change the city. He told me, "Of course not. Anybody who thinks he or she is going to change the city is going to end up very bitter." Then I asked, "Why do you stay?" "Steve," he replied, "I'm staying because God put me here."

When I was in seminary at Boston University, a number of students talked about the city and how they were going to serve there by changing social institutions. These students tried, but none stayed. In fact, many left the ministry altogether. Others finally opted for churches in the suburbs. Most, because we weren't given a secure belief system in seminary, graduated unsure that there was even a God, much less that He had called them to do anything. At Boston University, we "intellectuals" laughed at people like Doug who believed the Bible and loved God. We called them obscurantists and simpletons. We don't laugh anymore. Doug is still in the city, heading up a thriving ministry. He still believes the Bible and loves God. And I've joined his ranks.

At any rate, the interesting thing about the growth taking place in Boston under Doug's direction is that it's new growth. In many churches, much of the growth that occurs is old growth, where members transfer their membership from one church to another, or where young people from Christian families return home. There's nothing wrong with that kind of growth, but it does make me wonder why Christians and churches aren't penetrating the world and seeing some new growth—some non-Christians finding the Savior and joining His body on a local level.

I have a friend who, in preparation for a major film project, wrote to most of the major Christian media ministries in the country asking them to give him some statistics on how many people had found Christ through their ministry. When he compiled the statistics, he found that everybody in America had been saved some two-and-a-half times! I suspect that, given the number of pagans still around, many saved Christians have been "saved" many times over.

So I've been thinking about new growth recently. Maybe because of my conversation with Doug, or maybe because the Lord brought it to mind . . . or maybe because the Lord is using Doug to cause me to think about it. Whatever the cause, the questions my thinking have evoked are disturbing. Here are just two for you to chew on:

- Why aren't we making any major progress with hard core pagans?
- Why are so many people turned off by Christians and by our churches?

Of course, we can find some major exceptions—some places where Christians are making some important inroads into pagan strongholds. But let's be honest. Most people who come to Christ in our society are either already culturally "Christian" or have a predilection toward Christian things. That disturbs me.

We like to argue that our pattern of ministry came from Jesus. And while it's true that Jesus did establish a pattern of ministry we could (and should) emulate, I think that the places where we have ceased to make an impact have been where we established our own pattern of ministry and ignored or distorted Jesus'. For instance, we advertise great power and don't deliver. Jesus delivered great power and never advertised. I once saw a sign in a store that read, "All of the items on display here are not in stock." Unfortunately, that describes our lives far too often. When people find out we're Christians, they have a right to expect certain things. When they don't find them, they file it under false advertising, and rightfully so.

Author Ian Thomas has asked, "What is in your life right now that can only be explained in terms of the supernatural?" We can claim to have supernatural love, but it's only supernatural when one would expect hatred instead. We can claim to be forgiving, but forgiveness is supernatural only when there is no earthly reason for one to be forgiving. Compassion is supernatural when the smart thing seems to be to look out for number one. Freedom is supernatural when one would expect to be living in a prison. Joy is supernatural when circumstances don't warrant it. Integrity is supernatural when it's normal to define values in terms of one's own background and culture.

Nevertheless, as great as all this is, I really don't think that the major power of our witness is in our supernatural power and our righteousness. I think it has more to do with our honesty and vulnerability.

Jesus reached out to some very surprising people. He showed up in some very surprising places and He said some very surprising things. Unlike Him, we generally do what is expected of "religious" people. Being a "good citizen" is not the same thing as being a Christian, but in our society, *goodness* and *Christian* are used interchangeably. So church becomes the place where a nice, pleasant, bland person stands in front of other nice, pleasant, bland people urging them to be nicer, more pleasant, and more bland. Jesus didn't die to create nice, pleasant, bland people. He died so that sinners would find grace and forgiveness, and, in the joy and exuberance of their discovery, would find it impossible to keep quiet about it.

It's worth noting that Jesus didn't condemn bad people. He condemned "stiff" people. We condemn the bad ones and affirm the stiff ones. Whether it was a prostitute or a tax collector or an outcast . . . Jesus reached out to them. It was a motley crew of riffraff that followed Him around, and it never embarrassed Him or made Him feel uncomfortable. It still doesn't. But He's still angry at the "stiff" ones.

The great novelist Charles Dickens said in *Nicholas Nickleby*:

There are some men, who, living with the one object of enriching themselves, no matter by what means, and being perfectly conscious of the baseness and rascality of the means which they will use every day towards this end, affect nevertheless—even to themselves—a high tone of moral rectitude, and shake their heads and sigh over the depravity of the world.

78

Some of the craftiest scoundrels that ever walked this earth . . . will gravely jot down in diaries the events of every day, and keep a regular debtor and creditor account with Heaven, which shall always show a floating balance in their own favour.

That's the kind of people who make Jesus angry.

One of the most radical statements Jesus ever made is found in Matthew 9. We've sanitized it and made it fit our institutional molds, and thus allowed it to lose its power. I'm referring to these words of His: "It is not the healthy who need a doctor, but the sick. But go and learn what this means: 'I desire mercy, not sacrifice.' For I have not come to call the righteous, but sinners" (verses 12-13).

The difference between Jesus and us is that He didn't condemn the bad people—He loved them and understood them even though He would have been perfectly justified in condemning them. We, on the other hand, *can't* condemn the bad people because we are them. Therefore, our only alternative is to tell them, as fellow beggars, where we found bread.

I believe that one of the reasons the world isn't attracted to our religion and to our churches is because they think what we have is only for good people. Therefore, they think, it isn't for them. We have done a poor job informing the world that Christians aren't perfect, just forgiven and accepted and slowly getting better. Jesus said, "But I, when I am lifted up from the earth, will draw all men to myself" (John 12:32). If that isn't happening, maybe it's because we have been lifting ourselves up instead of Him. Maybe it's because we are giving the false impression that we're good people and that Jesus only loves good people. Maybe it's because we're flying under false colors—ours rather than His.

I love the story of the Anglican priest who saw an elderly woman who, because of the thought of her sin, shrank from drinking from the communion cup. The priest finally stuck it under the woman's nose and said, "Take it, woman! It's for sinners! It's for you."

I sometimes think about Doug and the great work he's doing. I'm convinced God is honoring Doug's work largely because Doug doesn't pretend to be something he's not. Doug is a sinner telling other sinners about a strange man hanging on a cross for them. That's dynamite stuff.

It's also a relief. I'm better than I was before I knew Christ, but my goodness still isn't enough to attract anyone to anything. But I can point to Him. People like Him a lot better than they like me anyway.

TIME TO DRAW AWAY
———— ❖ ————

Read Luke 7:36-50, Romans 5:6-11.

For meditation:

Did you ever think that your sinfulness could become
another person's invitation to accept Christ?
Don't get me wrong. I'm not suggesting that you should
flaunt your bad side. On the other hand,
trying to hide it is futile too; if you're like me, you know
that it keeps poking its head out at even the most unlikely
times anyway. So why not use it as an occasion to share
with a fellow sinner how he or she can find mercy and
grace for today and evermore as you have?

Ask God to give you just such an opportunity.
Then be on the lookout. He likes answering such prayers
because He doesn't "want anyone to perish,
but everyone to come to repentance" (2 Peter 3:9).

Dealing with the Past

This morning I received a letter from a man who had heard the Key Life broadcast in North Carolina. He's the owner of a radio station in Kings Mountain, and in the letter he said that he had heard me mention that I had once worked for radio station WPNF in Brevard, North Carolina. He said that he had built that station years before and wondered if I remembered some of the people he had known there.

Isn't it funny how an incident—the unexpected meeting of an old friend, a song, a particular smell or a letter—will trigger memories? It's sort of like opening a door to a room you haven't visited for a long time. You look at one thing, then another, and another. Pretty soon you're lost among all the memories that room recalls.

I'm not very big on nostalgia. (It's sort of like going into a bakery when one is on a diet—it smells good but that's all you get.) So I hardly ever sit down and consciously call up memories. I've always said that the past is past and that people who live in the past hardly ever do anything in the present.

But I suspect one of the major reasons I don't like to remember is because the pleasant memories are always mixed with some painful ones. Fused with the memories of friends, family, joy, and laughter are memories of failure, sin, hurt, and tears. Because you don't get the one without the other, I just let the dead bury the dead and keep on trucking. Memories are best left buried. And yet, they don't often stay buried. They blow away the dirt and rise up in our minds as either uninvited but pleasant guests or unexpected and unwelcome intruders, depending on what they make us recall.

Getting the letter from the station owner in North Carolina was one of those times. After reading it, all the memories surrounding that little radio station came cascading through my mind. It was a small slice of my past with so many good memories. For example, it was the time when I met and fell in love with Anna. I remember dedicating records to her during my show. I also remember the joy of learning the broad-

81

casting business, the awesomeness of the mountains, and the warmth of new friendships. I remember my first years of college there, and the discovery that, contrary to my previously held belief, I had a reasonably good mind and could think. I remember the life-changing experience of being elected president of the student government of the small college I attended. (It was no big deal. It was an extremely small class. One of us had to be president, but it was the first time I felt affirmed by anyone other than my mother.) I remember the crispness of the air and smell of hay on a hay ride.

But there were other memories too, and some not so pleasant. I remember the growing monster of doubt and the fear that people would discover that I wasn't what they thought I was. I remember the dread of failure and specter of shame and insecurity. I remember trying to pray and admitting, only to myself, that perhaps there was no one there to hear. I remember some people I hurt and some others I failed. I remember leading a campus revolt against a good and godly man and the horrible realization that I had hurt him deeply. I remember my intellectual arrogance and the inner disquiet over my future.

It was hard to stop the memories, but I didn't dwell too long on them. As I forcibly brought my mind back to the present, I remembered God. "Remember how the LORD your God led you . . ." (Deuteronomy 8:2). "Father," I prayed, "I don't remember much about You during those days. I didn't know Your name, and You seemed so far away."

The Father reminded me of the story of how little boys were initiated into manhood in one of the American Indian tribes. The small boy was taken from his family and led into the forest. He was told that he must spend an entire night in the forest alone. You can imagine the horror of it all. Every sound something to fear and every shadow a monster. But, as the sun would rise over the mountains, the boy's first sight would be his father. All night long, in the silence and just out of the boy's vision, his father had stood, bow and arrow ready, watching over and protecting his son. With incredible delight, the boy would run to his father, shouting, "Father, you were there all along!"

"Father, You have been there all along for me too."

God is, of course, the God of the present. I don't know how people who don't know Him deal with life. He is also the God of the future. To know Him is to trust the future to Him. But sometimes we forget that He is the God of the past as well.

82

The Bible teaches that God knew us and loved us before the foundation of the world (Ephesians 1:4). The Lord said to Jeremiah, "Before I formed you in the womb I knew you" (Jeremiah 1:5). The psalmist writes, "For you created my inmost being; you knit me together in my mother's womb. . . . My frame was not hidden from you when I was made in the secret place. When I was woven together in the depths of the earth, your eyes saw my unformed body. All the days ordained for me were written in your book before one of them came to be" (Psalm 139:13,15-16). Pretty incredible, huh? Even before God hung the stars, hollowed out the valleys, and made the mountains, we were on His mind. That means that every circumstance, every sin, every failure, every success, and every hurt was a part of His plan and love. That means that He knew me even before I knew His name. That means that He loved you before you were ever born. It means that when Christians remember, they don't remember the past; they remember the Father's dealings with them in the past.

I get a lot of letters from folks who have trouble dealing with the past. Some of the letters tell of sexual and physical abuse. Some tell of alcoholic, dysfunctional families, and great hurt. Others confess their secret sin and wonder if God could still love them. Some tell me about past failure and loss.

Perhaps the past haunts you sometimes. Perhaps there is pain there, and it hurts to remember. You don't have to live in the past, but if you are a Christian, you can remember, you can see His hand. You can accept the past because He has accepted you—past and all.

Isaiah, speaking God's word to God's people in a time of great travail, wrote:

"Remember these things, O Jacob,
for you are my servant, O Israel,
I have made you, you are my servant;
O Israel, I will not forget you.
I have swept away your offenses like a cloud,
your sins like the morning mist.
Return to me,
for I have redeemed you."
Sing for joy, O heavens, for the Lord has done this;
shout aloud, O earth beneath.

Burst into song, you mountains,
you forests and all your trees,
for the LORD has redeemed Jacob,
he displays his glory in Israel. (Isaiah 44:21-23)

He loves you. He really does. He always has and always will. When you remember, don't forget to remember that.

TIME TO DRAW AWAY
———— ✤ ————

Read Psalm 105, Ephesians 2:8-22.

For meditation:

*How has God shown His love to you? Take some time now
to recall and record past events that have demonstrated
to you that God is with you, protecting you, loving you.
Then turn toward heaven and thank Him for being by your
side and ask Him to keep on revealing His love for you
in even the small things of life. Don't worry.
He's more than willing to respond to this request.
After all, it fits with who He is, as John reminds us:
"God is love" (1 John 4:16).*

On Being Human

In a Charlie Brown cartoon, Charlie is eating a peanut-butter-and-jelly sandwich, and as he eats he notices his hands and becomes enamored with them. He holds them up and starts looking at them, then muses: "I like my hands. They are fascinating. They really are. I have nice hands. They have a lot of character. Do you realize that these two little hands may someday accomplish great things? These hands may someday do marvelous works . . . miracles. They may build mighty bridges, or heal the sick, or hit home runs, or write soul-stirring novels. . . ." Lucy finally interrupts this grandiose musing and puts it in perspective: "Charlie, your hands have jelly on them."

We need friends like that too—friends who don't worship at our altar. We're only human, not gods.

If you only have friends who think you're wonderful, they aren't friends. They're admirers. And admirers won't hang around long once they see the not-so-wonderful sides of your humanity. Lucy may sometimes seem to Charlie Brown as the bane of his existence, but she'll always shoot straight with him, and he—as well as you and I—need that.

TIME TO DRAW AWAY
———— ✣ ————
Read Proverbs 27:5-6, 28:23; Matthew 26:47-50.

For meditation:

Are your friends true friends or just admirers? Do they tell you what you need to hear or just what you want to hear?

What kind of friend are you? Are you willing to risk a friendship by telling the truth with gentleness rather than by hiding it out of selfishness?

*Inventory your friendships and your friendliness.
If you find one or both are out of balance,
seek God's wisdom to help you decide what you can do
to set the records straight.*

Are You a Manipulator?

While enjoying a party with some Christian friends a number of years ago, the door to the host's house flung open and in marched a woman nearly dragging her husband behind her. She made no attempt to quiet her voice as she announced, "George didn't want to come, but I told him we were coming anyway because I'd had a bad day." George, her husband, looked like the world had come to an end.

His outspoken wife first pulled him up to her, then pushed him off with the order, "George, mix." So George mingled. Not surprisingly, the farther away from her he traveled, the better time he seemed to have.

As George began to tell a story to some friends of his, it was obvious his wife was still keeping tabs on him. From across the room she yelled, "George, you're telling it wrong. I wish you could tell it right!" Then she pranced across the room and told the story he was trying to tell.

Later on in the evening, she humiliated him again by demanding, "George, it's time to go home. I need my sleep, and the children have been such pills today." And George followed her out the door.

Now I ask you, who was at fault here? If you answered, "George's wife as well as George," you were right. Apart from her unbecoming conduct, she was guilty of manipulating her husband from the moment he conceded to attend the party to the time they left. But George was guilty as well. Though it's a sin to manipulate, it's also a sin to allow yourself to be manipulated.

The art of manipulation is an old one. In the tenth chapter of the gospel of Luke, Jesus refused to accept the blame from what at minimum appears to be a manipulating woman. Jesus and His disciples had been invited by Martha to come into her home. But rather than join her sister Mary at the feet of Jesus and hear what He had to say, she became "distracted by all the preparations that had to be made" (verse 40). Upset that Mary wasn't helping her, Martha—acting like a martyr—went storming to Jesus and said, "Lord, don't you care that my sister has left me to do the work by myself? Tell her to help me!" (verse 40). Jesus' response is exemplary: "Martha, Martha, . . . you are worried and upset about many things, but only one thing is needed. Mary has chosen what is better, and it will not be taken away from her" (verses 41-42). Jesus was gentle, but please note that He didn't accept the manipulation and the guilt trip that Martha tried to lay on Him. And notice that He didn't do what she demanded ("Tell her to help me!"). Instead, He rebuked her and exonerated Mary.

Now lest you think I'm sexist, having brought up two examples of manipulative women, let me say something every man needs to hear. Nobody is a better manipulator than a man. Men have the ability to lay guilt trips on people that you wouldn't believe. The only difference between the way we do it and the way women do it is that we usually manipulate in a more subtle way. That way, fewer people know about it.

Let me tell you something you need to remember. It's a sin to manipulate. It's a sin to try to get people to be the way you want them to be by using low blows, guilt-inducing comments and actions, and the rest of manipulation's arsenal. It's a sin to say, "I'll stay here with the ironing and the washing and the dirty diapers and the bottles, while you go out to work everyday and have a nice lunch with all your friends." But let me tell you something else that's important: It's a sin to be the "manipulatee"; it's a sin to let others push you into their mold.

So how does one avoid manipulating or being manipulated? The same way one can avoid any other sin: by being set free from it through God's forgiveness and overcoming power.

I'll never forget the time in my life when I realized I was free of my sin. Because I was forgiven, I knew I didn't have to manipulate anymore. Likewise, if you find yourself trying to twist and turn everybody into your mold, get on your knees and say, "God, I want to be free of that. I don't want to be that way anymore. Let me know what it's really like to be forgiven." He'll take care of it, believe me.

On the other hand, if you find you're being manipulated because you don't want to make waves—you just want to smile and do whatever anybody tells you to do—you probably feel that way because you sense guilt. The solution for you is similar: Get on your knees and say, "God, let me know how free I really am!" God won't disappoint you either.

This is the way, the only way, to be free from manipulation.

TIME TO DRAW AWAY

———— ✛ ————

Read Romans 6:16-23, 12:1-2.

For meditation:

Write out as many manipulation techniques as you can. Then, honestly ask yourself which ones you may have used to get your way. Who got hurt in the process? From whom do you need to seek forgiveness? What can you do in the future to avoid being a manipulator?

Perhaps manipulation isn't your thing, but maybe you tend to fall prey to the manipulations of others. Can you identify some of the manipulative techniques that you usually fall for? Why do you permit them to get to you? You have a choice, you know. You don't have to give in. So what can you do in the future to avoid being manipulated?

Remember, no matter what side of this issue you fall on, you won't find real freedom unless you turn to God and ask Him to forgive and empower you. So don't leave Him out of the picture. If you do, it will only get ugly again.

Wounded, Yet Walking

Suffering is a fact. You can't escape it or excuse yourself from it. As long as you and I live in this world, we will suffer. But how can such misery be reconciled with the Christian view of God? After all, if God is omnibenevolent (all-good), wouldn't He want to rid the world of suffering? And if He's omnipotent (all-powerful), couldn't He eliminate it? But evil is still around. Why? That's a problem theologians and philosophers have tried to resolve for centuries. But when you're in pain, intellectual debate doesn't matter. You simply want relief.

So, when the pain becomes unbearable, and it will, how do you bear it? When you can't seem to cope any longer, how do you keep going? Christianity does have answers, and as strange as it may sound, they begin with One who knows suffering more intimately than you and I and the whole world combined. They begin with Christ.

Jesus suffered. First Peter 3:18 tells us, "For Christ died for sins once for all, the righteous for the unrighteous, to bring you to God." And then Hebrews 4:15, "For we do not have a high priest who is unable to sympathize with our weaknesses, but we have one who has been tempted in every way, just as we are—yet was without sin."

If God is in His Heaven, doing His thing, controlling the world, ordaining suffering, then I would be an atheist. However, if God is involved, if He somehow entered my world and pain to the point that He really knows what I go through and will do something about it, that's another matter altogether.

In his science fiction book *Perelandra*, C. S. Lewis introduces a character named Ransom, a philologist, who has gone to the faraway world of Perelandra to be God's instrument to deal with the prospect of a Fall on that planet. Ransom encounters evil personified in Dr. Weston, and it becomes quite apparent that ultimately the two will join in a battle to the death. As Ransom sits in the darkness of the night, he realizes that he must fight and that he might die. He thinks and prays. And out of the silence comes an answer to his prayer: "My name is Ransom, too."

If I were God (which I'm clearly not), and I asked you to do something I had not done, that would be one thing. If, on the other hand, I asked you to do what I have done, that is quite another. Jesus didn't come to keep you and me from suffering, hurting, and dying. He came to suffer as we suffer; He came to hurt as we hurt; He came to die as we will die; He came to live as we live. Since that's the case, how did Jesus deal with suffering and pain? Let's find out.

First, Christ suffered in submission. Look at Jesus in the Garden of Gethsemane, where facing His own death He prayed, "My Father, if it is not possible for this cup to be taken away unless I drink it, may your will be done" (Matthew 26:42). Our prayer every morning ought to be: "Father, I don't know what this day holds for me. I hope it is laughter and joy, but I know that it may be pain and suffering or hurt and humiliation. But whatever it is, teach me to accept it the way Christ did."

You see, there is no value in suffering per se, only in how we respond to it. Strike against it or become bitter by it and you will be bloodied. Accept it and you will become Christlike. Second, Christ suffered with the recognition that God's plan included it and gave it meaning. Did you notice the phrase, "if it is not possible" in the words we just looked at from Matthew's Gospel? In His prayer, Jesus recognized that within God's will, there is a reason and a purpose for suffering. You might ask, "All right, what is it?" That's a good question. Most of the time I simply don't know, but I know that God knows, and that is enough.

When our oldest daughter was little, she was extremely susceptible to strep throat. So almost every month she got another shot to deal with it. With her child's mind, she didn't understand antibiotics and shots. All she saw was a mean, old man with a needle that hurt. And the anxiety and hurt we felt, as parents, were even more than hers because we knew we couldn't explain it to her. No matter what we said, she simply wouldn't understand.

Pain has meaning if God is God. Sometimes God allows us to see that purpose—on a cross, in a lion's den, in a child's birth. But much of the time that meaning is hidden. That's when we need to pray, "Father, if it be possible, take the pain away. But if not, You are in control and You know why I must go through this. Help me rest in that."

Third, Christ suffered with the conviction that God was good and loving. If the meaning to suffering was wrapped up with a twisted God, we couldn't trust it. Jesus knew that wasn't the case. In Gethsemane, Jesus didn't address God as Jehovah or as supreme Ruler of the universe; rather, He prayed, "My Father." That makes all the difference.

The Christian social reformer Kagawa, when he was threatened with blindness and lay for months in the dark with terrible pain in his eyes, wrote:

Health is gone. Sight is gone. But as I lie forsaken in this dark room, God still gives light. At the center of things there is a heart. On yonder side of darkness there is light. To me all things are vocal. O wonder words of love! God and every inanimate thing speak to me! Thus, even in the darkness, I feel no sense of loneliness . . . In the darkness I meet God face to face . . . I am being born of God . . . I am constantly praising God for the joy of the moments lived with Him.

God *is* good, and He loves us always.

So what is suffering's purpose? How does God use it in our lives to bring about good? Suffering is the great purifier. As Peter states, "Therefore, since Christ suffered in his body, arm yourselves also with the same attitude, because he who has suffered in his body is done with sin. As a result, he does not live the rest of his earthly life for evil human desires, but rather for the will of God" (1 Peter 4:1-2). Suffering teaches, cleanses, and changes the believer who accepts it with the same attitude with which Christ accepted it.

By itself, pain is nothing but evil—it teaches nothing and cleanses nothing. However, pain borne with submission, recognition, and affirmation is different. Why? Because pain reminds us that we're mortal and teaches us to set priorities, to trust in God, to identify with the suffering of Christ, and to grasp lightly those things which are not eternal. Suffering is not wasted on those who follow Christ's example. Don't let it be wasted on you.

Thornton Wilder, in a short play, pictures a scene at the pool of healing. An angel troubles the waters and those who enter the waters are healed. A cripple, who has been waiting by the pool, rushes to the troubled waters only to find that his way is blocked by a physician who, with strong legs, can get there first. However, just as the physician is about to enter the waters, the angel stops him. The physician protests that the angel must surely understand his situation and need, but the angel remains strong in his refusal. The angel finally asks, "Without your wound, where would your power be?"

Without your wound, where would *your* power be?

TIME TO DRAW AWAY
—————— ❖ ——————
Read Isaiah 53, 1 Peter 2:20-25.

For meditation:

Are you struggling, hurting, in pain? Whether it's physical, emotional, mental . . . or you're suffering because someone you love is hurting, Jesus knows what you're going through. Share your feelings with Him, even if they're feelings of anger toward Him. He can take whatever you dish out. But don't stop there. Ask Him to give you the strength to endure and the peace to know that somehow, someway, He will use your suffering for good. Just as His suffering is bringing new life to untold numbers of hurting people, so He can take your suffering and transform it to bring about untold good for those in need, including yourself.

93

Forgiven and Forgotten

Right now you may be feeling guilty about one thing or another: what you said to your spouse last night, that last time you spanked the kids, those unrelenting immoral thoughts, something you did years ago and regret, actual lying and cheating. What do you do with this guilt? Do you try to ignore it? Bury it? Would you like to know how to handle it for good, how to find true forgiveness?

Let me give you an important principle for believers: *Definition is a prerequisite to recovery.* In other words, if you can define a problem, you can usually deal with it. Vague anxiety without definition of its source will simply wipe you out. It's important to define the problem before you do anything else. Let's define the problem of guilt based on Hebrews 10:1-18. Here we'll learn if forgiveness is even possible. So pause a few moments and read this important passage.

Did you notice that forgiveness has a requirement? To receive it, we must be sanctified, set apart to God. A lot of people try to make Christian principles work before they become Christians. When Jesus spoke to His disciples, one provision always followed upon the heels of His counsel: You must be a disciple of Jesus in order to reap the benefits of discipleship. When Jesus said, "My peace I give you"; "I have told you this so that my joy may be in you"; "Because I live, you also will live"; or "Surely I am with you always," He was only talking to a certain kind of person. Those are not universal statements applicable to everyone; they are meant only for His everlasting family. So, a word of caution: *Forgiveness is only for those who have gone to the only One who can forgive, Jesus Christ.*

Now take a look at the reality of forgiveness. The forgiveness Christ offers is the real thing; it's not a mere shadow or a copy. Let me illustrate what I mean. If I am really thirsty, one of the most arresting pictures I can see is a picture of a glass of cold water. The picture may be beautiful, it may make me think or daydream about a glass of water, but it is not a real glass of cold water. No matter how nice or realistic the picture, it is just that, a picture. In the same way, Christ's forgiveness really makes you clean and free. You are forgiven. That is reality.

Notice also the remedy toward forgiveness. Forgiveness doesn't come cheap; it never has and it never will. If I punch you in the nose and you decide to forgive me, that forgiveness costs something—a hurting, damaged nose. There's a sense in which all forgiveness is vicarious, substitutionary, one for another. Forgiveness always costs somebody something. In the case of the forgiveness offered by God, it cost Him His Son. Christ took your place. His death means that you don't have to die. Remember the cost.

In the Hebrews passage you can also see the reliability of forgiveness. "But when this priest [Christ] had offered for all time one sacrifice for sins, he sat down at the right hand of God" (Hebrews 10:12). Forgiveness is a fact because the One in authority, even Jesus Christ, says it is a fact. No data, no situation, no tragedy, no governmental decree, no military effort . . . nothing can ever change it.

There was a doctor in a mining town who had many patients who simply couldn't pay their bills. When they couldn't pay, the doctor wrote "Canceled" beside their debts in his books. Years later, when the physician died, his widow tried to collect on those debts by taking the past debtors to court. But the court replied, "If your husband said that their debt is canceled, it is canceled and can never be claimed again." Likewise, the King who rules has declared you "Forgiven." No one can change that fact.

See also that the reach of forgiveness is vast, "once for all" (verse 10). Jesus forgave every sin you have ever committed, every sin you are committing, and every sin you will ever commit. How about that? Corrie ten Boom described it, "Jesus takes your sin, past, present and future, dumps it in the ocean and puts up a sign that reads 'No Fishing.'" That is so true. Christ has given forgiveness as far into the future as our lives will reach. And He has given forgiveness into the past as far back as our lives have been lived. We really are free.

I know what you're thinking: *Well, does that mean I can do anything I want and I'm already forgiven?* Yes, that's what it means. *In that case, I'm going out right now to really sin, since it's forgiven anyway.* You may do that, but if you do, you haven't understood the motivation of love. I don't try to be obedient because He will zap me if I'm not. I try to be obedient because He loved me when I wasn't. I'm constrained by His love, not by His judgment.

Finally, also note the reminder of forgiveness. In Hebrews 10:17 God says, "Their sins and lawless acts I will remember no more."

There was a bishop who was a confessor for a nun. One day the nun told him that Christ had revealed Himself to her in person. The bishop, understandably doubtful about her vision, said to her, "I have some instructions for you. The next time Christ appears to you, I want you to ask Him about the sins of the archbishop." The nun said, "Of course."

So the next time, in a period of confession, the bishop said to the nun, "Well, did you ask Christ about the sins of the archbishop?" She said, "Yes, I did, Father." He replied, "Well, what did He say?" The nun answered, "He said, 'I've forgotten.'"

The living sacrifice of Jesus Christ has wiped your slate clean. God has forgiven your sin on the cross. Christ's death reminds us of that.

You may be on a guilt trip. I want you to think for a moment about the most horrible sin you have ever committed. Think about that which, if I revealed it over the broadcast or to your friends and family, would make you want to die. It may be a sin you've hidden for years, the one thing that nobody knows and you're never going to tell anyone about because you're so ashamed. Now hold it, in all of its blackness, before the light of Christ. Remember God's Word in Hebrews 10. He says this to you: "You remember your forgiveness and I'll forget your sin. You are free!" That's real. That's secure. That's yours—forever!

TIME TO DRAW AWAY
———— ❖ ————

Read Psalm 103, Ephesians 2:1-7.

For meditation:

Although you know you're forgiven in Christ,
you may still often feel guilty. It's during those times
that you need a reminder of the forgiveness that's already
yours in Him. To help you remember,
commit to memory a portion of one of the passages
mentioned in this devotional, or select another Bible text

*that would help you deal with this. If you have a hard time
memorizing, then write a passage on a card
or piece of paper and put it in a place where you'll see it
often. This should help you remember that you're really
free of your sin—past, present, and future.
Nothing is held against you anymore. Not one single sin.*

Hidden Agendas

A number of years ago I wrote a book with what, I thought, was a wonderful title. The publisher, though, didn't like the title I had chosen, so they selected one they felt was much better. I couldn't overrule them. When you sign a book contract, you sign your life away, and the publishers had the right to put any title they wanted on the book. However, publishers don't want to offend authors, and this one was no exception. They wanted me to agree that their title choice was a good one, even better than mine was.

At any rate, I was speaking at a conference in Kansas City, and one of the officers of this publisher flew to Kansas City to take me to dinner. I had never met him, and I thought that it was nice that he would go to that much trouble to meet me. He picked me up at the hotel in a very expensive car, he took me to a very plush restaurant (which was, incidentally, wasted on me, given the fact that the only use I have for food is that when you eat it you aren't hungry anymore and can then do something else that is really important), and he said some very nice things about me, my writing, and the ministry work in which I'm involved.

It wasn't until halfway through the meal that it dawned on me what was happening. (Most folks would have picked up on it sooner, but after all, I'm a preacher—it takes us a little longer.) "You turkey!" I said with great kindness. "Now I know why you have taken me to this fancy restaurant and why you are saying such nice things about me. You are trying to talk me into that title."

"Well," he said laughing, "that is a part of it, but I do like you."

His plan worked, by the way. The publisher used their title, and in retrospect, it was a good choice. I have, however, made it a general policy to disagree often with publishers. That way you get to go to some very nice places and have some very nice things said about you. I may be a preacher, but I'm not stupid.

The reason I relate this relatively unimportant incident to you is that it illustrates what most of us do in our relationships with people.

We deal with them with hidden agendas. Sometimes the agenda is as simple as our need to be liked. At other times it has to do with a business deal or an important favor we want. It would be naive to think that we could or should never take an agenda into a relationship, but we ought at least to be aware of it when we're doing it.

In most of Jesus' relationships with people, He didn't have a hidden agenda. His only agenda was love, and that was worn on his sleeve. He said, "Come to me, all you who are weary and burdened, and I will give you rest. Take my yoke upon me and learn from me, for I am gentle and humble in heart, and you will find rest for your souls. For my yoke is easy and my burden is light" (Matthew 11:28-30). On another occasion He said, "Greater love has no one than this, that he lay down his life for his friends. You are My friends" (John 15:13-14).

Most people are looking for favors, but Jesus was looking for a cross. Most people are trying to get something, but Jesus was trying to give something. Most people are harsh to people so they themselves will look better, but Jesus was harsh so that others might have it better. Most people are looking for acceptance, but Jesus was looking to accept.

Author Leighton Ford told me about a man who rented billboards all over Northern Ireland and put this message on them:

"I love you. Is that OK?"
Jesus

One time I heard Jerry Falwell speak to a national conference of conservative rabbis. He had a question-and-answer period at the end of his speech. One of the rabbis asked him, "Dr. Falwell, what do you want from us?"

Dr. Falwell replied, "I don't want anything from you. I have everything I want. I have come to say that I'm going to be your friend, even if you don't want me to be your friend. I've come to say that I love you, even if you don't want me to love you." He was saying that he had not come with a hidden agenda.

Did you ever think that a Christian is a person who should have no agenda except Christ? I know. That's hard, maybe even nearly impossible, but I believe that is what we are called to do. If Christ is Lord of everything, then those who belong to Him ought to have no agenda but Him. I don't mean by this that we should have no plans or that we should always be "religious" or "spiritual." I mean that a Christian, recognizing that Christ is the King, doesn't have to manipulate or coerce or shout or beat people over the head about anything. We are His property, paid for at a very high price. Moreover, He controls our circumstances, every encounter in every situation in which we find ourselves. So our question should never be, "What can I get out of this?" The only legitimate question is, "What does Christ desire in this situation?"

We do, of course, have agendas. It would be impossible to live without one. However, when we take our agenda and submit it to Christ's agenda, knowing that He never makes mistakes and that He loves us, we can enjoy a great sense of relief. We don't have to force or manipulate anything. We can simply enjoy the ride.

Did you hear about the man who lived in India and was required to take a rather long train trip to another city? He had his most valuable belongings packed in a suitcase which he placed in the rack above his seat. He told himself that it was important he stay awake to keep track of that suitcase. But during the night, for only a couple of minutes, he closed his eyes and dozed off. When he opened his eyes and looked up, someone had stolen his suitcase. To his amazement, he was relieved. "Thank God," he exclaimed out loud, "now I can go to sleep!"

We have, if we belong to Him, placed our important stuff in a suitcase. Jesus calls it the pearl of great price. Listen to His words: "The kingdom of heaven is like a merchant seeking beautiful pearls, who, when he had found one pearl of great price, went and sold all that he had and bought it" (Matthew 13:45-46, NKJV). We don't have anything to protect anymore. It's His, and He's watching it for us. So we don't have to have a hidden agenda. We don't have to manipulate people into the kingdom. We don't have to have folks think of us as wonderful people. We don't have to force people to do it our way. We don't have to make things come out right. We don't have to be successful or honored. All we have to do is be sensitive to His agenda for us and then be faithful to it.

You know, the best part of all this is that His agenda is always love. Within the context of His agenda, we will find forgiveness (when we fail and promote our own agenda), meaning (when we are looking for a reason to keep going), acceptance (when things don't turn out the way we expect), and a promise that in the end we will arrive safely home.

There, now, don't you feel better?

TIME TO DRAW AWAY
———— ❖ ————

Read 1 Corinthians 2:1-5, 2 Corinthians 6:3-13.

For meditation:

Reflect on the relationships you have right now—those in your home, at the work place, at church, at a favorite restaurant or health club. Are you carrying any hidden agendas into those relationships? Why? What do you hope to gain or escape?

Lay all your cards on the table before the Lord. Then let Him have them. Leave them behind. Let Him begin to transform your relationships and make you secure in Him and His plan, rather than in yourself and your plans. Then watch how well He works. You'll be amazed, and so will the people to whom you relate.

How to Make Your Problems Worse

Have you ever faced a problem and then tried to solve it, only to make it worse? I have too. And you know, we're in good company. Jesus' hand-picked twelve disciples managed to fall prey to the same problem. Perhaps by seeing what they did, we might learn how not to solve a problem. Our story is a familiar one: It's where the disciples find themselves in the middle of a storm out at sea, and they begin to wonder if they're going to survive it (Mark 6:45-52). Let's check it out.

The first mistake the disciples made was thinking that Jesus was unaware of their problem. Picture the scene. The disciples are trying to go against an incredible head wind and not doing very well. As far as they know, Jesus is still with the crowd they had left, doing His own thing, unaware of what's happening to them. In reality, though, that's not the case: "When evening came, the boat was in the middle of the lake, and he was alone on land. He saw the disciples straining at the oars, because the wind was against them" (verses 47-48). Jesus was well aware of their situation, and He is of ours, too. Don't ever forget that.

Not too long ago, I received a letter from a girl who had been through the terribly tragic situation of a suicide in her family. In part she wrote:

> To get to the point (whatever it is) I am so lonely, I'm getting to the point where I'm almost panicky with depression. I feel alone, alone, alone. And grief is about the only emotion I possess apart from an unexplainable anger. I feel hateful and hated.
>
> Last night my mother told me if she had it to do over again, she wouldn't have any kids. She was serious. And I don't blame her. I wish she hadn't, too.

Do you know what I told this girl? I told her how the psalmist said that when your parents kick you out, the Lord takes you in. I told her that even if she didn't sense it, and even if she didn't know it, Jesus Christ was aware of everything through which she was going. That's true for you and me also.

The second mistake made by the disciples was that they actually thought their problems were worse than they really were. The gospel of Mark says that it was the fourth watch—between 3 and 6 a.m.—before Jesus went into the sea to do anything about the problem. In other words, Jesus sat on the mountain, looked at the storm and the disciples struggling in it, and He didn't do anything about it for hours. In fact, "He was about to pass them by" (verse 48). Jesus knew the problem was not as bad as the disciples thought it was. He looked at them and knew they were having trouble; He knew they were having to row hard. But that was good for them. He knew they were not going to go down.

A man was walking across a railroad trestle during a very dark night, and horror of horrors, he heard a train coming and had no place to go. So the man jumped to the side of the bridge and held on to the trestle's edge. When the train finally passed over him, the man found he didn't have the strength to pull himself up and knew he was just going to have to hang there. If not, he feared he would fall into the abyss thousands of feet below. That morning, in the light of day, the man found he was hanging only six inches from the ground.

We're like that, aren't we? Jesus said if you have just a little bit of faith, you can move mountains. Now that's hard, but let me tell you something: It's much easier to create mountains, and we're good at it. I build mountains all the time. If I get a stomachache, I'm sure it's cancer; if I get a headache, it's some kind of tumor; if my hand begins to tremble, Parkinson's is on the way. We all do that. Someone once said, "Fear knocked at the door, faith answered, and nobody was there."

The third mistake: The disciples confused the solution with the problem. When they first saw Jesus walking on the water, the disciples mistook Him for a ghost and were terrified. Sound familiar? Let me explain.

One of the most important principles any Christian can ever learn is the principle of praise: "Give thanks in all circumstances, for this is God's will for you in Christ Jesus" (1 Thessalonians 5:18). That means no matter what happens to you, give God the praise. How? You can do it because He is involved in every circumstance of your life.

A little boy went to his grandfather and said, "Granddaddy, do you ever really, I mean really, see God?" His grandfather answered, "Son, I sometimes think that's all I see." As Christians, we need, as Brother Lawrence says, to practice the presence of God, then we won't be so afraid when He shows up.

If you want to make your problems worse, see every problem as an accident. If you want to make your problems better, learn to see God's hand in them. Learn to listen carefully and you can hear Christ's words, "Take courage! It is I. Don't be afraid" (Mark 6:50).

Fourth, the disciples made their problems worse by failing to realize that Jesus had the power and the willingness to still the storm. I don't know about you, but I'm glad Jesus Christ controls the winds, whether they be financial, physical, or spiritual.

One of the reasons our problems are of such great proportion is that we insist on staying alone in a leaky boat while we put band aids over the holes. Our band aids are usually in the form of "If I only."

- "If I only had another $1,000 a month."
- "If I only had a nicer house."
- "If I only had better clothes."
- "If I only had a psychiatrist."
- "If I could only get married."
- "If I were only single."
- "If I only had a different spouse."

If all our "If I only's" only came true, then, we tell ourselves, everything would be all right. But it never is and never could be, because they're not the solution to our real problem. Our real problem is that Christ isn't in our boat to stop those terrible head winds. We haven't asked Him to come alongside us and help. Or, we've sought His advice, but we're unwilling to take it. We're still convinced that we can handle our overwhelmed boat on its own. But we can't, so the winds keep blowing, harder and harder.

A while ago, a couple of my friends did a great thing in their Sunday school class. They gave each child a little plant to take home. Every day the kids were to read their Bibles and pray; then, and only then, could they water their plants. Think about it. If the kids didn't read the

Bible and didn't pray, the plants wouldn't get the water they needed and they would die. As they saw what happened to their plants, depending on what course they followed, the kids also saw what happened to their souls and to their lives. When Jesus Christ is in the boat, He takes care of the winds and the leaks.

Finally, the disciples made their problems worse simply because they refused to let past victories deal with present panic circumstances. Look at the end of the story. After Jesus climbed into the boat, the wind died away. The disciples "were completely amazed, for they had not understood about the loaves; their hearts were hardened" (Mark 6:51-52). Get the picture: The disciples had just seen Jesus feed five thousand people with five loaves and two fish. Jesus kept breaking the bread and passing it until everyone had their fill and twelve full baskets were left over. Can you believe it? Later that same day the disciples were so frightened about the storm that they never imagined that Jesus would come to their rescue if they really needed it or only asked. This is a classic example of a very short memory. And we understand it all too well, don't we? Our hearts harden too, when we forget about past circumstances and past victories.

Remember the story in Joshua 4? God told the people of Israel to take twelve stones out of the middle of the Jordan River, and take twelve stones from the side of the river's bank, and put them in the middle of the river as an altar. Why? So when their children would ask, "What do those stones mean?" they could answer, "It reminds us of the time when God dried up this river bed so His people could safely walk across it." You ought to be doing that with your life rather than following the disciples' example of failing to allow past victories to inform present panic situations.

Life is like an ocean, and we're the sailors. Sometimes there are storms; sometimes there are leaky boats; sometimes there seems to be no way out. The appropriate prayer for a sailor is, "O God, Thy sea is so great, and my boat is so small." That is more than enough. God will handle the rest.

TIME TO DRAW AWAY
— ❖ —
Read Exodus 14, Acts 12:1-18.

For meditation:

What are your "If I only" solutions? Are you willing to lay them aside to ask Christ to come alongside instead? Remember, He's in the business of doing "immeasurably more than all we ask or imagine, according to his power that is at work within us" (Ephesians 3:20). So don't be afraid to trust Him. Rather, be afraid not to trust Him!

No Super Christians

After a week of meetings in Pittsburgh, a man came up to meet me following the last service. A former missionary and member of the church for over thirty years, he said something to me I still haven't been able to classify as either a compliment or something otherwise. "Steve," he said, "I've really appreciated what you've said this week." I told him I was glad. Then he added, "I've been in church all my life, and all my life I've heard pastors say that they were sinners. You're the first one I ever really believed."

Though I still chuckle about that remark, I acknowledge with complete sincerity his observation. You see, I'm not a pastor and radio preacher because I'm good or have abilities or because I'm talented. I'm where I'm at because God put me here. And sometimes I'll be soft and sometimes I'll be hard, but you remember, I'm just like you. God must remind me over and over that even when people call me Reverend, I'm not. Christ established an equality in the brotherhood that has direct implications for me as well as you.

In every congregation of believers, God sets aside brothers and sisters who are called of God to lead. But the problem is, sometimes we get the idea that we are God's gift to the world, and when that happens, the delicate balance between gifted leadership and ecclesiastical elitism gets shattered. There's no room in the Body of Christ for elitism of any sort. That's the world's way.

After Queen Victoria and Prince Albert had had one of their famous, loud arguments, Prince Albert went to his room and slammed and locked the door. Queen Victoria marched after him and pounded on his door.

"Who is it?" asked Prince Albert.

"It is the Queen of England."

Dead silence. Then again the question: "Who is it?"

"It is your sovereign ruler," replied the Queen.

Then once again, "Who is it?"

"It is your wife, Victoria, Albert."

At that point Albert opened the door.

You may be an elder or a deacon or a leader in your Sunday school. Perhaps you lead in some of the other groups in your church and conduct Bible studies. Whatever your role, I thank God for you. But remember that you're doing it (or at least should be) because God told you to do it, not because you're a super Christian. There are no super Christians in the Body of Christ. All of us are just one among equals. So when a Christian brother or sister stands on the pedestal of his or her status . . . when the peacock feathers start flying in the breeze . . . don't bow. That kind of behavior doesn't need to be encouraged. Honesty does. The importance of being honest and acknowledging our true condition and coequal status cannot be overstated.

When a Christian gets honest, something exciting happens. We get to the point where God can use us. Evangelist D. L. Moody once said, "I've had more trouble with D. L. Moody than with any other man I've ever known." Thomas à Kempis said, "Be not angry that you cannot make others as you wish them to be since you cannot make yourself as you wish yourself to be." If we don't get honest with ourselves, then God is going to force it on us.

Let me tell you a prayer that God always answers: "Lord, show me myself." Don't pray it unless you mean it because He will surely answer you, and you won't like what you see. But He'll make you different through it—I guarantee it.

Super Christians? They don't exist. There are only sinners saved by the blood of the Lamb. Remember that next time you find yourself enjoying compliments so much. If you listen carefully, you will hear them sound like a cape flapping vainly in the wind.

TIME TO DRAW AWAY

—————— ❖ ——————

Read 1 Corinthians 3:3-23, 12:1-27.

For meditation:

How are you doing on the equality scale? Let's find out. Complete the statements on the left-hand side of the chart by checking off one of the categories in the right-hand section of the chart that seems to best describe your situation.

I LIKE . . .	USUALLY	SOMETIMES	RARELY
flattery	❑	❑	❑
winning	❑	❑	❑
my way best	❑	❑	❑
center stage	❑	❑	❑
getting even	❑	❑	❑

If any of your answers landed in any of the columns, then welcome to the club of sinners, where everyone stands on the same platform, whether they sin rarely, sometimes, or usually. Keep that in mind, regardless of how high you seem to be climbing on the leadership or popularity ladders. We're all equal in Christ—as sinners saved by His blood, as servants saved by His blood, and as leaders saved by His blood. No exceptions.

Honesty

I'm bald. I don't like it. I wish it weren't true, but it is. For years I tried to hide it; I combed my hair just the right way to cover it up, at least a little. I also used to hate to have my picture taken because the photographers always managed to arrange the lights so I appeared bald. A friend who loves me said, "Steve, the reason you look bald in those pictures is because you are bald." Horrors. But you know something? I finally accepted the reality of my baldness, and now, to be honest with you, it isn't half bad.

Our sin is like that. We deny it, we pretend it isn't true, we cover it by pointing at someone else's sin. And then God tells us the truth: "There is no one righteous, not even one" (Romans 3:10). You're a sinner. And so am I. With that settled, we can be honest with one another.

God hardly ever grows hair on a bald head, but He does make us better if we are honest about being sick. You think about that.

TIME TO DRAW AWAY
—————— ❖ ——————

Read 2 Samuel 11:1–12:13, 1 John 1:8-10.

For meditation:

When was the last time you were really honest with God,
when you didn't try to cover up your feelings or thoughts
or motives or wrongful actions with piety?
Whether it was yesterday or a year ago, don't wait any
longer. He knows you're a sinner saved by His grace.
You don't have to try to hide that from Him.
So go ahead, be honest. That's the first step
to healing and transformation.

God Knows Your Limits

I once counseled a man who, as a small boy, had been punished by his father. The father had hit the boy because of some kind of childhood indiscretion. The problem was that the father had not stopped, and what started as an action of correction became an act of incredible abuse. The boy ended up in the hospital. When I talked to him years later, he hated his father. In fact, he hated most people, and those he didn't hate, he didn't trust. I had to be careful when I spoke of God as Father because this man knew only an abusive father. I didn't want him to think that the heavenly Father was like his own earthly father.

Maybe you struggle with God as Father too. Perhaps your past is filled with abusive treatment that makes it difficult for you to conceive of any kind of father figure as good and loving. Or, maybe you've come under the disciplining hand of the Father and you feel He's harsh and unkind. Let me tell you, it's true that God chastens His children. If He didn't, He wouldn't really love us. But listen: He knows when to stop, He's always fair, and He never disciplines out of spite or selfish motives.

TIME TO DRAW AWAY
❖

Read 2 Chronicles 7:11-14, Hebrews 12:7-11.

For meditation:

Are you feeling the sting of God's discipline because of sin in your life? If so, and you feel as if His punishment never stops, the problem isn't with Him— it's with you. He is a kind and loving Father, whose arms are always open to the broken and the contrite sinner. So the question is, Are you really repentant, or are you still harboring rebellion? Only you and He can answer that question, and only you and He can resolve it.

111

Supernatural Life

A friend of mine told me a great story the other day, which he confirmed was true.

A woman shipped a very valuable dog on an airplane. But when the clerks checked the cage after the flight was complete, they found the dog dead. So they went out and bought one just like it and replaced the live dog for the dead one. When the woman came to pick up her dog, she looked in the cage and stepped back in surprise.

"What's the matter?" an attendant asked.

"Why," she said in a trembling voice, "that dog was dead when I put him in the cage."

Jesus said that Christians have passed from death to life. Since that's true, pagans, especially those who knew us before we trusted in Christ, ought to be just as surprised when they come in contact with us as that woman was when she saw her dog. Our new life ought to be different than the old dead one—so different, in fact, that people notice the difference.

What in your life can only be explained in terms of the supernatural? Ask a pagan. He should know.

TIME TO DRAW AWAY
———— ❖ ————
Read Acts 9:1-31, Ephesians 4:17–5:12.

For meditation:

What habits of your old life still linger in your new?
I know. Old habits die hard, but God is bigger than any
habit, and He sure won't tolerate bad ones.
So get tough with them. With God at your side, start
rooting them out of your life. As long as you rely on Him,
you can do it—He promises you (Philippians 4:13).

112

Looking for Me

I once looked for me after I had been in an accident. My car had overturned and I had escaped without a scratch. I was standing on the side of the road with the onlookers when a hero-type pulled off the side of the road and ran down the hill to the crumpled car and started looking for me, the driver. He was sure someone had been killed. After helping him look for me for a while, I laughed and told him that I was the driver of the car. To say the least, he was not very happy with me. He told me in no uncertain terms that what I had done was a horrible way to treat someone who was trying to help. He was right, of course.

God helped me look for me too. The Bible says that in my lostness, God sent His only Son to find me and bring me home. I knew I was lost, and I was looking for a way out. Then He came and rescued me and restored me to Himself.

I'm working at treating Him better than I did the man who tried to help me after my car accident.

TIME TO DRAW AWAY
— ❖ —
Read Psalm 119:169-176, Luke 15:1-7.

For meditation:

*If God has found you and saved you from the wreckage of
a godless life, thank Him by following Him in all He wants
you to do. Remember, too, that He wants you to scour
the wreckage of the lost and tell whoever will listen
that there's a way out, that Someone wants to rescue them
if they will only trust in Him.*

*Do you know someone who needs Him? Pray for them,
then go and tell them about the Rescuer. He's looking
for anyone who will listen.*

113

PART•TWO

HITTING
GLITCHES

If you've ever done much work on a computer, you know about glitches. "Oh, no!" and "NOOOOO!" and "Heeelllp!!" and "Don't do that, I beg you!" are common among workers who have just had their computer screen go blank, or their disk drive mysteriously erase three just completed and critical files, or noticed their fingers hit the wrong command key to the demise of their spreadsheets. Sometimes the comments are more descriptive, and they usually come when the pressure is at its peak. See if you recognize any of these—personally:

- "It ate my document!"
- "Where did that file go? It was on screen a second ago."
- "We're out of printer paper again?! And we've got to FedEx this tonight! What are we supposed to do, cut down our trees and make our own paper?"
- "If my mouse acts up one more time, I swear I'm going to feed it to my cat!"

Glitches have a bit more bite to today's office worker because everything we do is so fast-paced. We do "word processing," not typing. We FedEx almost everything. If we really want to do something quickly, we fax it or shoot it to someone through a modem. And with all these hyperfast contemporary conveniences come a whole new generation of glitches.

Now glitches aren't new, nor are they peculiar to the high-tech office environment. Farmers face glitches when equipment doesn't operate right or breaks down at harvest time. Moms deal with glitches with kids, pets, shopping, and a slew of other potentially nagging or unexpected problems. But people make it through these difficulties.

You can too.

Hitting glitches is just part of life. Everyone faces them—those daily challenges that don't seem like enormous hurdles, but rather trip us up and irritate us, much like someone sticking her leg out in front us just to watch us stumble a bit before we catch our balance again. If we can just keep our perspective intact, we can keep ourselves from letting these nuisances get to us. But that takes a little preparation, so we're going to do some of that in the following devotions.

Keep in mind, God is with you, even through the minor glitches and strange little riddles of life. Nothing is too small for our big God to know and handle.

CHAPTER THREE

DAILY CHALLENGES: THOSE TYPICAL GLITCHES

❖

*But we have this treasure in jars of clay to show that
this all-surpassing power is from God and not from
us. We are hard pressed on every side,
but not crushed; perplexed, but not abandoned;
struck down, but not destroyed. . . . Therefore we
do not lose heart. Though outwardly we are wasting
away, yet inwardly we are being renewed day by day.
For our light and momentary troubles are achieving
for us an eternal glory that far outweighs
them all. So we fix our eyes not on what is seen,
but on what is unseen. For what is seen is temporary,
but what is unseen is eternal.*

Paul the apostle
2 Corinthians 4:7-9,16-18

There's a Place Where Winter . . .

I don't want to rub it in or anything, but for you who live in the cold north country, southern Florida is a wonderful place to spend February. The summer isn't that great, but February . . . now that's a good time to be warm in Florida.

Sometimes when I see pictures of snow in a magazine advertisement or on postcards (usually with a farm house and pine trees bent over with the snow), I miss the places where I have lived. The mountains of North Carolina and New England still hold a very special place in my heart.

But then I remember that those places aren't really like the postcards. I remember the cold, the ice, and the dangerous driving. (In the snow, I'm one of those drivers who cause accidents. I go very slowly and always in the wrong lane.) I remember going to the basement in our home in the mountains and praying there would still be a spark in the coal furnace from the night before. I remember shoveling the snow and working all week on a sermon only to have no one to hear it because of the big snowstorm. I remember trying to get warm after we had lost our electricity and spending hours bundling up our daughters only to find out from Anna that I had gotten their boots on the wrong feet and three coats and two sweaters on backwards.

When I told Anna we were moving to Florida, she could hardly believe it. Every time we had moved before, it had been farther north. She fully expected that the next place we were to serve Christ would be Alaska. But even in Florida, I don't think she has ever been fully warm. (She says that when she dies she wants to be cremated because it will be the only time she was ever warm enough.) And so February is a nice time to live in Florida.

There is a wonderful old hymn by John Newton that Frank Boggs sometimes sings. (Frank says that the reason I like his singing so much is that if I did sing, I would sound like him. When we get to heaven, Frank is going to have to preach, and I'm going to be the soloist.) Let me share some of it with you:

How tedious and tasteless the hours,
> When Jesus no longer I see.
Sweet prospect, sweet birds, and sweet flowers,
> Have all lost their sweetness to me,
The midsummer shines but dim;
> The fields strive in vain to look gay:
But when I am happy with Him,
> December's as pleasant as May.
Dear Lord, if indeed I am Thine,
> If Thou art my sun and my song,
Say, why do I languish and pine,
> And why are my winters so long?
Oh, drive these dark clouds from my sky.
Thy soul-cheering presence restore;
Or take me unto Thee on high,
> Where winter and clouds are no more.

I remember the first winter we moved to Florida. It was a sad time because we were leaving a lot of people we really loved. I thought I would die. We drove through New York City in the middle of a snowstorm. I remember taking our two little girls and putting them in an airplane at La Guardia so they could spend those difficult moving days with their grandparents in the mountains. It was very cold; driving was dangerous; I could hardly see because of the snowstorm. Anna was flying in from Boston and the girls were flying out from New York. And there I sat in the airport, probably the loneliest and coldest preacher in America.

Do you know what sustained me during those days? The people in Florida had written us dozens of letters welcoming us to our new church. In those letters they wrote, "We can hardly wait until you guys are here." One man said, "The temperature is eighty degrees and I'm going fishing. The next time, you will go with me." A lady sent us a postcard with a picture of palm trees and a sandy beach. You see, I was miserable, lonely, cold, and afraid. But I knew that if I just held out a little longer, I would be in the sun and fun of Miami.

Heaven is like that. We live in a fallen world, and sometimes things are so bad that we can't stand it. This world is not a wonderful place. So we long for something better. Our permanent home. Heaven.

I believe that you need to understand what the Owner's manual (the Bible) has to say about how we should live and how to go about it. But my ultimate goal is to get you home joyfully with faithfulness to Christ as your crowning achievement.

Earlier I talked about how we need to be heavenly minded to be of any earthly good. But did you realize that it's possible to be so earthly minded that you forget where home is? One time John Wesley was being shown around the estate of a very wealthy man. He looked around and commented, "These are the things that made it difficult for a man to die."

What I've been doing through the radio ministry is sort of like telling someone in a snowstorm about an even better place than Florida in February. A place where winter and clouds are no more.

I've been thinking more about Heaven recently. A lot of my friends are already there. Because of Christ, you are going to be there too.

Sometimes we need to be reminded.

TIME TO DRAW AWAY
———— ✤ ————

Read Luke 12:13-34, 2 Corinthians 5:1-10.

For meditation:

Do you treat this life as your home, or are you living as if heaven is your real home? What do you think a heavenly minded life would look like? Does yours mirror those qualities, those distinctives? Give these questions some serious thought, then decide with the Lord what you need to do about your answers.

If You Want to Know About Dealing with Worry, Ask a Worried Man

Did you hear about the epitaph on the tombstone of the perennial hypochondriac? It read, "I Told You I Was Sick!"

I don't know about you, but I'm a worrier. In fact, when I'm not worried, I'm really worried. Every headache is a brain tumor, every letter from a lawyer is a notice of a lawsuit, and every noise on an airplane is the precursor to a wing falling off. Of course, I've never had a tumor, been sued, or been in a plane accident. But that doesn't mean that I won't, and that worries me.

You say, "You've got to be kidding, Steve. If you're that bad, maybe I'll listen to someone else on this subject. You of all people shouldn't be talking about how to handle worry any more than you ought to be selling a cure for baldness. When you stop worrying and grow hair, then come back to me with your cures."

Wait. Before you stop reading, let me ask you something: Would you ask a contemplative monk about how to raise children? How about asking a member of the women's temperance union how to deal with a booze problem? Would you go to a car mechanic who had never had car trouble? Of course not. So if you want to know something about how to handle worry, I'm probably, of all your friends, one of the best to ask. In the absence of fear, there can be no courage. Just as courage can be defined only in the context of fear, freedom from worry can only be defined in the context of worry. If you want to know about dealing with worry, ask a worried man.

I'm glad you asked. Let me tell you what I've learned about overcoming worry.

First, when I'm worried, I try to remember the difference between a problem and a fact. Let me give you an important truth a friend taught me a long time ago: A problem is something you can do something about, and a fact must just be accepted. Jesus said, "Who of you by worrying can add a single hour to his life?" (Matthew 6:27). Not one of us. There are some things that just are, and if there's no solution, then there's no problem because a problem is something you can fix. When I'm worried about something, I say to myself, "Myself, what do you propose to do about this problem?" If I can't find an answer, I don't have a problem—I have a fact. At that point I ask God for the grace to accept what I can't change.

I love psychologist Robert Eliot's statement: "If you can't fight it or flee it . . . flow with it." That's good. Remember it. Change what you can; flow with what you can't.

Second, most of my greatest worries come from the fear of facing the reality of whatever it is that worries me.

I once visited a friend of mine in the hospital whose honesty was wonderful. Most of the time when I visit hospitalized Christians and ask them if they are worried, they say something spiritual like, "No, Steve, the Lord has given me His peace. I'm trusting in Him, and He has given me the assurance of His love and control." Now I'm not saying that kind of statement is never true. Some Christians (the ones you don't want to ask about worry) have a wonderful gift of trust. They just don't worry. However, I suspect that sometimes those kinds of folks are practicing what the psychologists call "denial." At any rate, I asked my friend if she was worried. She said, "Worried? Are you crazy? Of course I'm worried. People die in this place!"

Isn't that refreshing? And you know, God dealt with her worry because she was honest about it, identified it, and thereby knew how to pray about it.

People often ask me if I'm so afraid of flying (which I am), how I manage to get on airplanes. I tell them two things: First, I know exactly what worries me—people die in airplanes; second, because I've identified my worry, I can talk to the Father about it in very precise terms. When I'm specific with Him, He is specific with me.

There is a wonderful English proverb that I've found helpful: "Fear knocked at the door. Faith answered. Nobody was there."

Third, my anxiety level lowers when I recognize that while the things I am worried about just might happen, nothing is going to happen that doesn't first pass through the nail-scarred hands of my elder Brother, Jesus.

Don't you hate those people who tell you not to worry because nothing will happen? I don't know how many times I've heard this, but I've verified it through experience: "I said to myself that things

122

couldn't get any worse. But they did." I may be unable to control my circumstances, but He isn't and He does and He loves me. "And we know that in all things God works for the good of those who love him, who have been called according to his purpose" (Romans 8:28). "For from him and through him and to him are all things. To him be the glory forever! Amen" (11:36).

Fourth, I face worry with the understanding that I'm valuable to God. You know, I think the greatest source of our worry is the fear that nothing we do and nothing we are is valuable.

Someone gave me a book the other day called *Children's Letters to God*, compiled by Eric Marshall. One of those letters reads: "Dear God, If you do all these things you are pretty busy. Now, here's my question. What is the best time I can talk to you? I know you are always listening, but when will you be listening hard in Troy, New York? Sincerely Yours, Allen." Jesus would say to that little boy, "I always listen hard because you are valuable to Me."

Jesus reminds us that we are important. No matter what happens to us, our every prayer is heard, our every tear is counted, and our every hurt is noted. That is what the cross is all about. At the very center of God's heart is His Son's cross, and it's there because of His tremendous love for us. What better way could He express our great worth?

Fifth, in dealing with worry, I try to remember the principle of priority: Put first things first, and secondary things will take care of themselves.

I taught swimming for a long time. There was one little boy, Billy, who wanted to dive. I went over all the steps of diving, telling him, "Son, when you get your head right, everything else will take care of itself." He would do a belly flop into the pool, swim over to the side, and ask me, "Were my hands right?" I would say, "Don't worry about your hands. Worry about your head." He would mess up again and then ask, "Mr. Brown, were my feet together?" I would say, again, "Don't worry about your feet, Billy; worry about your head. If your head is right, the rest will be right."

The Christian walk is just like that. Get the priorities straight and let God worry about the rest. And what are the priorities? They're no secret; Jesus told us: "Seek first his kingdom and his righteousness, and all these things will be given to you as well" (Matthew 6:33).

What are your priorities? What are you seeking first in life?

Family? Money? A successful career? There's nothing wrong with those things, but if your priorities are anything but God's Kingdom and His righteousness, everything else will be out of whack. Put God's priorities first, then everything else will take care of itself.

Finally, I deal with worry by realizing that most of the things I worry about really won't happen. Jesus said, "Therefore do not worry about tomorrow, for tomorrow will worry about itself. Each day has enough trouble of its own" (Matthew 6:34).

My worry is a matter of trust. My prayer is not so much for a change of circumstances (though sometimes it is) but for the gift of trust. There's a direct correlation between the degree of my trusting Christ and the level of my anxiety. Once I recognize that, I ask for the grace to trust in Him no matter what.

The current state of the economy is bad and will probably get worse. That worries me. I worry about the Middle East and the people I love who are there. I worry about my family and about bills. I worry about living, and I worry about dying: The good news is that you are going to heaven and the bad news is that you are going on Thursday. I worry about Key Life and my faithfulness. I worry about the Christian church in America. I worry about politics and philosophy. I sometimes worry about the lack of values in our society, and the people's lack of concern for the things of God. Mostly I worry at night. Sometimes God comes and says, "Steve, no use both of us staying awake. You go on to sleep."

It was a very steep, winding mountain road. The tourist bus inched its way down, navigating the curves with great care. Then the bus driver and tourists smelled the burning brake shoe against the drum of the wheel just before the brakes gave way. The bus rapidly picked up speed. The anxious looks of the passengers, occasionally punctuated with the screams of two people toward the front of the bus, increased. But far in the back of the bus, a little boy had fallen asleep, and no matter what happened, he remained asleep.

When the bus finally reached the foot of the mountain in one piece, everyone expressed great relief and gratitude. One man woke up the little boy, told him what happened, and asked him in a laughing way how he could possibly sleep through such a dangerous ride.

"Sir," the little boy said, "I could sleep because my father drives the bus."

Our Father drives the bus too. No matter how bad the road, regardless of how worrisome it becomes, we can sleep. He's never had an accident, you know.

He told me to tell you that. Have a good night's rest.

TIME TO DRAW AWAY
❖

Read Psalm 37, Matthew 6:25-34.

For meditation:

What are you worried about? Finances? Job? Kids? Husband? Wife? Illness? Death? Whatever it is, the Lord wants to help you handle it. Determine the source of your worry, then follow the steps for dealing with it laid out above. I know He'll come to your aid. Take it from a fellow worrier.

Celebrities

I'm always glad when famous people come to know Christ and tell others about Him. But sometimes it worries me, because sometimes the impression is left that if the famous sports player, singer, or actor knows Jesus, then people can rest assured that Jesus is okay.

Instead of Jesus validating an individual (as it should be), the individual validates Jesus. Now I'm sure the celebrity doesn't mean for that to happen. But as a society, we're so awed by celebrities that their conversion becomes greater news than the One who converted them. Listen to something important: Jesus doesn't need any help with His credibility, but we need a lot of help with ours. Celebrity conversions are great; they need Christ too. But let's never forget among all the hoopla who it is that does the saving.

Jesus Christ reaches out to people where they are: in the movies, on television, in sports, politics, business, the home. Wherever they are and no matter what they're doing, without Him they are all helpless, afraid, and lost. Yes, He seeks to win celebrities too, not because they're famous, but despite the fact they are. That makes me glad. If He didn't operate that way, He would never have noticed me.

TIME TO DRAW AWAY
———— ❖ ————
Read 2 Kings 5:1-13, Luke 19:1-10.

For meditation:

Do you devour news about celebrities?
Do you buy, believe, or discourage things because
of what famous people say and do? What does
a celebrity-focused mind-set say about someone's values
and attitudes? How might it impact yours?

Christ is the only "celebrity" we need. Rather than exalting the famous, why not begin praying for those you admire? Make Him and His values and His attitude the center of your focus. Someday, some lost celebrity may thank you.

Criticism

 M ost of the time, you ought to ignore criticism. After all, your enemies will believe it before they hear it; your friends won't believe it after they hear it; and most folks will never hear it anyway. But there are some things that just won't go away unless you deal with them.

I heard about a pastor who was criticized because he supposedly went to a meeting his wife was attending and forced her to leave. In self-defense, he took out an ad in the local newspaper, which read:

In the first place, I never attempted to influence my wife as to her choice of a meeting.

In the second place, my wife didn't attend the meeting in question.

In the third place, I did not attend the meeting.

In the fourth place, neither my wife nor myself had any inclination to attend the meeting.

In the fifth place, I do not now have, and never have had, a wife.

Confrontation is sometimes important. If you ever have to confront your critics, just make sure you do it with gentleness and love.

TIME TO DRAW AWAY
——— ❖ ———
Read Proverbs 9:7-9, Ecclesiastes 3:7.

For meditation:

Have you come under verbal attack lately? Are you dying to strike back? Or are you so flustered by it that you're not sure what to do?

*Whatever course of action you decide to take,
consult the Father about it first. He's had to deal with this
problem a lot through the years. If anyone's ever been
wrongly criticized, He has. And His Son even died at the
hands of His critics. So talk to the One who knows.
He'll guide you well.*

Chastening

When I was in grammar school, I had a principal named Mr. Brown. He was one of the hardest disciplinarians I have ever known. I was in his office a lot. It wasn't that I couldn't be good; I just couldn't be good long enough. Those were the days when principals were allowed to administer a firm hand to the backside of an undisciplined boy. I had felt his hand on numerous occasions.

Many years after I left that school, a friend of mine told me that he had met Mr. Brown. My friend told me, "He said you were one of his favorites." *Well,* I thought, *he sure had a funny way of showing it.* Then I remembered the verse: "The Lord disciplines those he loves" (Hebrews 12:6).

I didn't really like being one of Mr. Brown's favorites, but I'll tell you something, I'm glad he didn't ignore me either. That would have been much worse.

TIME TO DRAW AWAY
❖

Read Proverbs 12:1, 15:31-32.

For meditation:

What would your life be like if God had ignored you, if He had decided to let you go your own way without ever intervening? Pretty frightening thought, isn't it?

Now consider someone who may be under your care who needs you to intervene. Are you willing to step in? Do you love them enough to rebuke, to discipline, to do the hard thing?

God wouldn't give up on you. Perhaps it's time for you to do the same for someone else.

130

Loneliness

When Prince Albert died, Queen Victoria made one of the saddest statements I have ever heard. Her words were uttered through her tears: "Now there is no one left to call me Victoria."

Loneliness knows no bounds in the human family. It strikes queens and kings and commoners alike. That is why, when God calls a person, He calls him or her not only to the throne but to a family—the family of God.

"People who need people are the luckiest people in the world," the song proclaims. But the lyrics don't go far enough. The fact is, people who need people are the *only* people in the world.

The Body of Christ is supposed to be the place where people know the names of the family members. A part of the work of Christ is to introduce Christians to Christians—by name. The church should be the one place where everyone knows your name, where no one has to go it alone. I know that isn't always the case, but it can be and it ought to be and the solution begins with you and me.

TIME TO DRAW AWAY
——————— ❖ ———————

Read Philippians 4:21-23, 3 John 13-14.

For meditation:

Whether you're feeling lonely or lonely people
are around you, the solution is the same:
You need to step out and greet someone.
Don't wait for someone else to make the first move;
it may never happen. Besides, the person you greet may be
just as lonely as you, and he or she may be waiting
on someone just like you to extend a welcome hand first.
So go ahead. Take a chance. All you've got
to lose is loneliness.

131

Mistakes

John H. Holiday, who was the founder and editor of *The Indianapolis News*, stormed into the composing room one day, determined to find the culprit who had spelled *height* as *hight*. A check of the original copy indicated that he had been the one responsible for the misspelling. When he was told that he said, "Well, if that's the way I spelled it, that has to be right." For the next thirty years, *The Indianapolis News* misspelled the word *height*.

How difficult it is for us to admit our mistakes, and how much easier it would be on us and others if we would.

I have a friend who drove twenty miles in the wrong direction to keep from admitting to his wife that he had taken a wrong turn. (Well, actually, it wasn't a friend; it was me.)

Being sinners in a fallen world means that we are all going to be wrong a lot. That's okay . . . as long as we're honest about our mistakes.

TIME TO DRAW AWAY
───── ❖ ─────
Read Genesis 12:10-20, Ephesians 5:25-27.

For meditation:

You know, it takes more energy to conceal a mistake than
it does to admit one. And more often than not,
once you admit your error, any terrible repercussions you
thought you would have to face aren't nearly as bad
as you had imagined. So why don't you get it over with?
If you're wrong, get it off your chest.
You'll breathe a whole lot easier.

132

Doing Our Best

Once while speaking at the National Press Club, President Eisenhower told his audience that he regretted he didn't have a better political background and that he was not more of an orator. He said his lack of these qualities reminded him of his boyhood days in Kansas when an old farmer had a cow for sale. The buyer asked the farmer about the cow's pedigree, butterfat production, and monthly production of milk. The farmer said, "I don't know what a pedigree is, and I don't have any idea about butter fat production, but she's a good cow, and she'll give you all the milk she has."

God doesn't ask you to be something more than you are, but He does ask you to give the best you have. I find that comforting. I can't give anymore than I've already got anyway.

TIME TO DRAW AWAY
———— ✥ ————
Read Deuteronomy 30:11-20, 2 Corinthians 9:6-15.

For meditation:

Are you really giving God your best?
Is there anything you're holding back that He deserves?
Remember, if you're in Christ, you're the Father's;
you no longer belong to yourself. So all that's yours is His.
Is He receiving His due?

Pride

I had dinner with a friend in West Virginia who was a relatively new Christian at the time. As we walked into the restaurant, he pointed to a nearby mountain and said, "Steve, when we sit down, I'll tell you what I did on that mountain."

Once we were seated, he told me that a few months before he had stood on that mountain with the enthusiasm of a new believer. His enthusiasm wasn't shared by everyone, though, so as he stood there, he said to God, "Lord, I'm the only one left who wants to do Your will."

I asked him, "What did God say to you?"

He laughed and replied, "God said, 'You've got to be kidding!'"

Arrogance and pride have no place among the people of God. No matter how good or bad, how committed or uncommitted, how enthusiastic or unenthusiastic, we come to the cross with nothing. Anything we receive after that we get from Him. That's quite humbling, as well it should be.

TIME TO DRAW AWAY
—————— ❖ ——————

Read 1 Kings 19:1-18, Proverbs 16:18-19, Galatians 6:14-16.

For meditation:

What do you have worth boasting about before God?
If it's anything other than Him and what's He's done
for you through Christ, then it's too much.
Call it what it is—empty pride—and confess it before Him,
seeking His forgiveness.

Perfectionism

She was only twenty-six years old. She was an outstanding Christian, working as a professional in a church. After college she had served for a year on the mission field. I didn't know her well, but I liked her a lot. She was a strong witness for Christ, and she was an articulate spokesperson for evangelical Christianity.

This morning I got the message that she'd taken her life. I was absolutely devastated. Not only that, I didn't understand.

As if that were not enough, shortly after hearing about her suicide, I got a call from a man who listens to my radio broadcast. "Steve," he said, "I haven't told anybody in the world what I'm going to tell you. I have decided to leave my wife, and I told God that if I get through to you, I would do whatever you told me to do."

I asked him what prompted him to decide to leave her.

He told me, "I became a Christian at fourteen, and all my life I've been living up to the expectations of others. I work full-time in a ministry, I teach the Bible, and everyone thinks I'm the model Christian. I'm just tired of it. I've decided to do something for myself for a change."

Let me share a letter with you I received a couple of weeks ago. There was no return address, and the person gave me no name.

> Dear Stephen,
>   Please pray for me as I am on the edge—a total failure as a Christian. I have failed as a husband and as a father. He [God] has probably given up on me. I feel so very alone and abandoned. It's a horrible feeling that words alone cannot describe. Please don't judge me. Pray for me.
> Sincerely,
>   The Lord knows who I am

At first these three incidents didn't seem related. They were just about individuals for whom I had prayed. But in the silence of my prayer, it dawned on me that they all had the same problem: They all had created a false standard of perfection (or accepted someone else's standard), and they couldn't live up to it.

What advice would you have given them? If you had talked to the young lady before her suicide, or the man thinking about leaving his wife, or the anonymous correspondent—what would you have said?

Most people would say they should try harder. The problem is that all three already had.

Some would suggest they pray and read the Bible more. But they all had done that too.

Others would tell them to receive Christ and have faith. But, you see, all three had received Christ. And yet, they discovered that the faith they needed can't be turned on and off like a faucet.

And then there are those who would send them to a mature Christian who would then tell them to try harder, read the Bible, pray, and have faith so their witness would not be hurt.

But what would Jesus have told them? We don't have to guess: "Come to me, all you who are weary and burdened, and I will give you rest. Take my yoke upon you and learn from me, for I am gentle and humble in heart, and you will find rest for your souls. For my yoke is easy and my burden is light" (Matthew 11:28-30).

Perfectionism is a horrible disease. It comes from the pit of hell, smelling like rotting flesh. Someone convinced these folks that they were called to measure up to a perfect standard. They couldn't do it, and each in his or her own way simply quit trying.

Nobody told them that Jesus was perfect for them, and because of that they didn't have to be perfect for themselves. They didn't understand that if Jesus makes you free, you will be free indeed (John 8:36).

They never heard—or if they did, they didn't understand—that Christians aren't perfect, just forgiven, accepted, and loved and getting better. Someone should have mentioned that if God was satisfied with them, nobody else had the right not to be.

I told the man who wanted to walk away from his wife about God's unconditional love. Do you know what happened? He started crying. And before we got off the phone, he had decided to do the right thing. Not because he had to but because he was responding in freedom to the love of Christ.

Nobody can help the young lady who took her life, that is, nobody but Jesus.

And what about the correspondent? Without a return address and a name, only Jesus can handle that one too.

What can we do? We can present and model the real Jesus—the One who came to lift our burdens, not to add to them the hellish weight of perfectionism. Perhaps we could then see fewer sacrifices on the altar of perfectionism.

TIME TO DRAW AWAY

——— ❖ ———

Read 2 Corinthians 3:17-18, Galatians 5:1.

For meditation:

Do you find yourself caught in a performance trap,
where no matter what you do it doesn't seem to be enough?
Is a standard of perfection driving you further and further
into despair and depression? Please listen carefully: That's
not God's standard or expectation; it's someone else's.
God doesn't enslave His sons and daughters;
He frees them and enables them to serve.

Don't keep trying to measure up to a standard that's
not His. If need be, get some outside help, but take serious
steps to cut the shackles holding you down.
Oh, what a relief it will be!

Uneven Playing Fields

Have you noticed how much of the news media slants stories? For instance, if you are pro-abortion, you are called pro-choice. If you are pro-life, you are called anti-abortion. The unborn baby is called a fetus, abortion is just another medical procedure, and the determination of when life begins is established by public opinion polls. Sometimes the news media really angers me.

But then I remember that the playing field wasn't even for Jesus either, and His followers have been playing on a slanted field ever since. Uneven fields should never surprise Christians; we should expect them. Jesus, after referring to how He had been treated, said that the world would treat us the same way and that we shouldn't be surprised. Then He added, "But take heart! I have overcome the world" (John 16:33).

No, the playing field isn't even, and I know Jesus warned us about it, and we shouldn't expect things to be different. But . . . well . . . it still makes me angry.

TIME TO DRAW AWAY
———— ❖ ————
Read 2 Chronicles 36:11-16; John 15:18-16:4,33.

For meditation:

What's your particular uneven playing field right now?
Or are there many? Identify them.
Understand that in this life you will always be on uneven
ground. But remember, Jesus is the great equalizer;
He can help you overcome the imbalance because He has
overcome all the obstacles.

So take your cares and anger to Him. He'll help you know
how to handle matters from there.

138

New Year, New Land

January first always marks the beginning of something new. With the new year looming in front of us, we don't know what will happen. So we face it with anticipation, fear, and excitement.

The people of Israel experienced something similar as they went into a new land, the Promised Land God had pledged to them (Joshua 1:1-9). What God told them then will help you when you face new years, new lands, new ventures. So listen well.

First, as you enter something new, remember something about the past. Take a look at what God told Joshua, the one who was assigned to lead the Hebrew people into the Promised Land He'd given them: "Moses, my servant, is dead. Now then, you and all these people, get ready. . . ." You may think that was a small thing, just the passing of leadership from one good man to another, but remember that for forty years Moses had been a father to Joshua.

For forty years, when Joshua was frightened, didn't know what to do, and had a major decision to make, he went to Moses. For forty years when things had fallen apart for Joshua, he could turn to Moses to help him put the pieces back together. Now where was he going to go? His mentor was dead; the great leader of God's people was gone. Joshua's grief and sense of loss must have been great. But God told him to get up, to move on.

Maybe this past year has brought a divorce in your life. Maybe you've lost someone you loved deeply. Maybe you've done some bad things that you feel really guilty about inside. Maybe you haven't been faithful the way you know you should have been. But God tells you to get up and get ready to move ahead. Remember the past? Yes. But then put it behind you. This is your year. As the Apostle Paul said, "One thing I do: Forgetting what is behind and straining toward what is ahead, I press on toward the goal" (Philippians 3:13).

Second, remember something about the promise. In Joshua 1:3, God said, "I will give you every place where you set your foot, as I promised Moses." Not a bad promise. "Joshua, every place where you put down the leather, that will be yours." God had promised that the land was for His people, and He reiterated that promise to Joshua.

Paul says that as God's people, "All things are yours . . . and you are of Christ, and Christ is of God" (1 Corinthians 3:21-23). Before God ever hung the stars and hollowed out the valleys, He thought of you, called you to Himself, and made you one of His people. Before you were ever born, He planned the life that you would live. You are a daughter or a son of the King.

As you walk through the year, don't wring your hands and whine. It is your life, and it is your year. You go out in the name of the God of the universe and face your future.

People are always coming to me, feeling guilty, without joy, and lacking meaning in their lives. Let me ask you something: If you were forgiven, how would you act? You are forgiven, so go and act that way. If you had meaning or joy in your life, how would you live? God has given you those things, so go and live that way. In the taking of the land in the coming year, the reality of God's promise and provision will become existential in your life. "Fake it until you make it" is an abomination for a pagan, but for the one who belongs to the God of the universe, it is simply acting on the reality of the promise He has made to His people. The One who has the right to promise and the power to keep it has promised.

Third, as you enter something new, you need to remember something about the power. Look at Joshua 1:5-6: "No one will be able to stand up against you all the days of your life. As I was with Moses, so I will be with you; I will never leave you nor forsake you. Be strong and courageous."

A man went into a hardware store with a chain saw. He threw the saw down at the store owner's feet and said, "That is a piece of junk. You told me that I could cut down forty trees a day, and I couldn't cut down any more than three."

The owner replied, "Well, maybe the teeth on the saw need to be sharpened."

Once that was done, the man took the saw back home, only to return three days later with almost the same complaint: "This is still a piece of junk. It's a little bit better, but not much. Now I can cut down only five trees a day, and you said I could cut down forty. I really want my money back this time."

"I really don't understand it," replied the store owner. "This is a good piece of equipment. Let's try it." The owner pulled the starter cord and the chain saw started right up.

The man looked at it, surprised, and said, "What in the world is that noise?"

We're like that. We have the chain saw, but we haven't found out about the power. I believe most Christians live empty lives simply because they don't realize that all the angels of God are poised to listen to their words. You need to draw on God's power; it's your greatest resource.

Fourth, remember something about the procedures. Joshua 1:7: "Be strong and very courageous. Be careful to obey all the law my servant Moses gave you; do not turn from it to the right or to the left, that you may be successful wherever you go."

When my wife and I first went to Boston, she was pregnant, we had no money, and I needed a job. With a voice that sounds like a foghorn, I walked into a radio station, one of the major markets in those days. As it turned out, the program director had just lost his production manager.

He said to me, "I ordinarily wouldn't even talk to you, but can you do production?" You need to know that I couldn't even spell *production* in those days, but I still answered, "Can I do production? I'm your man."

Then the manager took a commercial and gave it to me. It was a complex radio commercial for dog food—a dog balancing a can of dog food on his nose in a circus with the drum rolls starting, with applause, and with a detailed script. The manager asked, "Well, can you do it?" I said, "Can I do it? I'm your man."

He hired me on the spot as his new production manager—a young man who had never done production.

During the following two weeks, I bought every book I could find on production. I read each book very carefully and analyzed every sentence. For me, this job was a bottom-line situation; I simply had to have it and make it work.

You and I are in exactly the same situation now. In our lives, bad things are going to happen and opportunities we had never considered are going to challenge us. We'd better, then, stay close to the Owner's manual.

An absolute God has given you some absolute standards by which to live. Make sure you study and apply what God teaches in His Word. He tells you where the mine fields are, and He points the way to the Promised Land. Make sure you understand the procedures He gives so you won't blow it.

Finally, while looking ahead to something new, above all, remember something about the presence. As God told Joshua, "As I was with Moses, so I will be with you; I will never leave you nor forsake you" (Joshua 1:5).

One time when my daughter Jennifer was a little girl, she came to me and asked, "Daddy, you're always talking about how God speaks to you and how you listen to God. Well, I've been listening real hard, and I haven't heard Him. How do you know God speaks to you? How do you hear His voice?"

My temptation was to get out a book of systematic theology, share it with Jennifer, and intimidate her to the point where she wouldn't ask that question again. But as a parent, I felt called by God to answer with His help. And thankfully, He helped on that occasion. I said, "Jennifer, you remember the girl in your class who's the new student? You told me last night how lonely she looked. She didn't have any friends and you felt really sorry for her."

"Yes, I remember, Daddy."

"Do you remember when you first came to Key Biscayne and you were new at school?" I asked. "You were the only kid who didn't have any friends."

"Yes, I remember."

Then I added, "You connected those two things, didn't you? You told me last night that you were going to be that little girl's friend. Who told you to do that?"

After a long silence, Jennifer smiled and said, "Oh . . . so that's Him."

Don't forget as you move on to something new to move with the presence of the God of the universe.

TIME TO DRAW AWAY
————— ❖ —————
Read 1 Samuel 3, John 16:5-14.

For meditation:

How do you feel about what lies ahead? Are you anxious or excited or afraid or simply uncertain? Whatever your feelings, take them before God. Rest in His presence and promise. Then move out with the confidence He provides. He won't let you down . . . really, He won't.

Being Helpless

Do you ever feel helpless? I can identify with the fifty-year-old pastor who said, "When I was young I prayed that God would allow me to win the world for Christ. When I was thirty I prayed, 'Oh, God, may I win my city.' When I was forty I prayed, 'Lord, let me win the people in my church.' And now I pray, 'Lord, help me not to lose too many.'"

Someone has said that the man or woman who is not liberal before the age of thirty has no heart, and the man or woman who is not conservative after the age of thirty has no brain. (I don't know if I agree with that given the fact that I am just to the right of Genghis Khan and have been from the moment of my birth.) When you're young, there's no problem that can't be solved, no mountain that can't be climbed, and no challenge that is too big to accept. But as you get older (and some folks get older sooner), you begin to realize that some problems exist that just don't have solutions. Do you remember what Matthew said about Jesus' visit to Nazareth? "He did not do many miracles there because of their lack of faith" (Matthew 13:58). Even Jesus hit some stone walls now and then.

I sometimes feel helpless. I'm concerned with the hole in the ozone layer (and even feel guilty about it sometimes), but I can't fix it. I worry about the economy and want to help out, but I don't even understand what the GNP is, much less what to do to make it better. I worry about what those turkeys are doing in Washington, about the energy crisis, about mass starvation in parts of the world, and about the homeless. But I feel so helpless.

I teach a men's Bible study here in Miami, and after I started writing this devotion, I had to set it aside to go teach that Bible study. I was rather irritated to have to do it. But do you know what the text we studied was? Matthew 14:13-21. It records the time when Jesus fed the five thousand in spite of the helplessness of the disciples.

Do you remember the incident? Jesus was in a desert place with over five thousand people, and those folks were hungry. Then Jesus told

His disciples to feed them. When the disciples looked for food, they found that in the entire crowd they could find only five loaves of bread and two fish. Talk about helpless! There wasn't a Burger King down the street and no bakery where they could hustle up a couple thousand loaves of bread to make sandwiches or something. The text doesn't say it, but the disciples are friends of mine, and I know what they said: "You've got to be kidding! We can't possibly feed five thousand people with this little food."

Then, in the face of their helplessness, Jesus did what they couldn't do: He fed the crowd, every last hungry person. "They all ate and were satisfied, and the disciples picked up twelve basketfuls of broken pieces that were left over. The number of those who ate was about five thousand men, besides women and children" (verses 20-21).

One of the men in my Bible study told us about a large wood-frame hotel here in Florida (he said that it was the largest in the world). The hotel was made out of Florida pine, and just one match in the wrong place would create the largest pile of Florida pine ashes in the world. So the engineers designed and installed a very expensive and elaborate sprinkler system to protect the place. A few years ago they were adding to the hotel and found out that the sprinkler system had never been hooked up. So as great as it was, it would never have helped avert a disaster because it had never been connected to a water source.

Connecting the system to the source. That's how the Christian deals with helplessness.

During the Bible study we started talking about the areas where most of us were worried and felt helpless. We found that we felt helpless about our businesses, our families, our physical problems . . . and on the list went. Do any of these items sound familiar? They're not much different than those things you feel helpless about, are they? Then we began to remember those areas in the past where we felt helpless and where God had intervened just as Jesus had in feeding the five thousand.

When we finished the Bible study, all of us felt a little better, not because we were less helpless, but because in our helplessness we remembered that we could trust God who is never helpless or without resource.

The American folk religion says, God helps those who help themselves. I suppose there is some truth to that. But what do you do when you can't do anything? How do you help yourself when you have no strength left? Where do you turn when you simply don't have the resources to meet the needs you have? The Bible says, God helps those who *can't* help themselves and who know they can't.

We all feel helpless at times, and for good reason—we are helpless. (Did you hear about the psychiatrist who was counseling the man who had an inferiority complex? He said to the man, "Sir, the reason you have an inferiority complex is because you are inferior.") There are so many problems and needs in our lives for which we have no remedy, so many mountains that are too big to climb, so many challenges we can't meet. A feeling of helplessness is the rational response to reality.

But we aren't totally helpless, are we? There really is a God. He really is sovereign over every circumstance. He really did give us His Son as a propitiation for our sin. He has really forgiven us and accepted us. He really does love us. He really does want what is best for us. We really can trust Him. All we have to do is make sure that the sprinkler system is connected.

One time Spurgeon was worried about his ministry in London and the resources he needed to maintain it. He was depressed and filled with anxiety. Then God brought to his mind a rather silly image. It was the image of a mouse in the granaries of Egypt under Joseph. The mouse was worried about enough to eat. Then Spurgeon thought about a fish in the Thames river and how worried the fish could get about having enough water to breathe.

Then Spurgeon began to laugh: "Eat away little mouse," he said, "there is plenty. Swim away, little fish, there is more than enough water." And then, addressing himself, he said, "Stop worrying, little man. God has enough and more!"

TIME TO DRAW AWAY
———— ✤ ————

Read Psalm 121, Hebrews 13:6.

For meditation:

*Feeling helpless about anything? The first step to change
is to check your connection to your best source of help.
Is it firm? Any leaks? Solidify the connection,
then let Him infuse you with His strength and peace.*

146

Judging People

Have you ever had your opinion changed about someone by observing one incident? Maybe you thought someone was an abrasive, sullen, intimidating turkey, and then that person did something that caused you to radically change your opinion.

Well, that's happened to me. I know a man I love to dislike. Whenever I thought of him, I saw him as the personification of the kind of meanness one sometimes sees in Christians. Then my brother died, and I met this man at a conference. He came up to me and said, "Steve, I want you to know how sorry I am about your brother's death, and I wanted you to know that my wife and I are praying for you each morning." *Lord,* I said silently, *couldn't You leave me with at least one person I could hate?*

One time, when I offered to introduce a man to someone else, he told me, "I don't want to meet that man. If I knew him, I might like him. And I don't want to like him."

Oh, how much we miss when we judge others.

TIME TO DRAW AWAY
———— ❖ ————
Read Proverbs 14:21, Matthew 7:1-5.

For meditation:

Are you holding someone at arm's length because you don't
want to get to know him or her? Why?
What's holding you back? Are you guilty of judging them?
If so, ask God to forgive you. He will.
Then hold out your hand to this person in welcome.
You may be surprised at what you'll find.

CHAPTER FOUR

RIDDLES OF LIFE: THOSE SPECIAL GLITCHES

❖

God is [either] the greatest of fantasies or the greatest of facts. Those are the only two possibilities. . . .

Why are we so reluctant to admit this eminently logical truism with respect to God, though not with respect to anything else? Because it means that one of the two sides, either the believers or the unbelievers, have been basing their entire lives on the most fundamental illusion that has ever bedeviled humanity. . . .

How could anyone be indifferent to this question? If God equals only Santa Claus for adults, who in his right mind would want to believe in such a myth all his life? If God equals the heavenly Father, who in his right mind would want to disbelieve in his own father?

Peter Kreeft
Does God Exist? The Great Debate

Getting What You Want

I was in a bookstore the other day and a clerk came up to me and said, "Can I help you?"

"I don't know what I want," I answered. "But when I find it, I'll let you know."

Most of us are like that. We're really not sure what we want. And even if we stumbled onto what we thought it was, we would probably find out that it wasn't what we wanted anyway.

The most unhappy person in the world is not someone who didn't get what he or she wanted. The most unhappy person is the one who got what he or she wanted and then found out that it wasn't as wonderful as expected. The secret of a happy life is not to get what you want but to live with what you've got. Most of us spend our lives concentrating on what we don't have instead of thanking God for what we do have. Then we wake up, our life is over, and we missed the beauty of the present. You think about that.

TIME TO DRAW AWAY
❖

Read Ecclesiastes 2:24-26, 4:7-8.

For meditation:

What do you really want out of life? In your pursuit of it, are you missing anything along the way? Could you even be missing greater joys? Don't treat these questions flippantly. Your answers will reveal a lot about what you hold most dear, and what your answers don't include may tell you what you're missing in the process.

Is the pursuit really worth it?

Systems

We Christians are big on systems. There are the ten steps toward a happy marriage, the five ways of knowing God's will, the eight commandments for raising children, the six steps to developing an effective prayer life, the twelve steps to recovery.

I have a lawyer friend who is a Christian and who read a book on prayer. "Steve," he said, "I thought that my problems with prayer were due to my not knowing the system. So I read this book, learned the rules, then determined that now I could really pray. So, I went to my office early, got out my book, and began to pray. It was the worst prayer time I ever had."

He forgot that God is not a system. He's a person.

Did you hear about the young man who read a book on lion training? When he finished reading it, he sneaked into the lion cage at the zoo. The next morning, the zoo's attendants found a torn book and a full lion.

Systems have their place, but they can never replace relationships or personal experience. If you want to know God intimately, put the systems (and books) down and spend time with Him.

TIME TO DRAW AWAY
---- ❖ ----

Read Ecclesiastes 12:11-14, John 5:39-40.

For meditation:

You and I both know that you can read parenting books until you're cross-eyed, but until you become a parent, your true education hasn't begun. The same applies to learning a job, a craft, a sport, a musical instrument . . . virtually anything in life. So why do we think our relationship to the Lord is any different? Yes, we need to know His Book, but if that's all we know, we don't know enough—our true education hasn't begun.

Do you know Him, or just His Book? Get together with Him. Get reacquainted. Start today, and make it a daily habit. You don't need a system—just time, desire, and the willingness to listen.

Friends

A friend of mine got into a terrible fight with another friend over a three million dollar contract. That happened a long time ago, but its effects still linger. My friend told me recently, "I got a bad deal. I would give up the money to have my friend."

If you ever have to make a choice between money and friends, always choose friends. They last a whole lot longer.

A man who was blind from birth was asked what he thought the sun looked like. "The sun looks like my friends," he replied.

Rev. Charles Kingsley was asked the secret of his long and productive life (1819–1875). He referred to scholar and educator F. D. Maurice and said simply, "I had a friend."

We used to sing a song: "Make new friends but keep the old, one is silver and the other gold." We've changed that in our society: Make new friends but discard the old, one is useful and the other's cold. That's sad.

The Apostle John said that friends ought to be greeted (3 John 14). The church ought to be a fellowship of friends. It would make a tremendous difference, wouldn't it?

TIME TO DRAW AWAY
— ❖ —

Read Proverbs 17:17, Ecclesiastes 4:9-12.

For meditation:

What kind of friend are you? Are you there when your friends need you? Do you really love at all times?

Are there any tears in your relationships that need mending? If so, why not take the first step? That would be the loving thing to do.

Atheism

I once had dinner in Israel with a man who said he was an atheist. The interesting thing about this man is that he led his family in the ancient Jewish prayers during the evening meal. That didn't compute with me. I had not earned the right to ask him about his behavior, so I remained silent. But I would have liked to have asked him why he prayed if he didn't believe there was anyone there to hear him. That seemed quite inconsistent to me. But then, as Emerson said, "Consistency is the hobgoblin of little minds."

The next time you know an atheist well enough to ask questions, ask why, if there is no God, he or she believes that love is better than hate or that kindness is better than anger. The answer, I suspect, won't be very consistent. Sort of like people praying to a God they don't believe is there.

TIME TO DRAW AWAY
❖

Read Psalm 14:1-6, Isaiah 44:6-23.

For meditation:

If you know any atheists (people who disbelieve in the existence of God) or agnostics (people who aren't sure whether a God exists), consider the way they live and how it matches what they say they believe. You'll be amazed at how far apart their beliefs and actions really are.

By the way, how consistent are you?

154

Belief

I won an argument once with a pagan. He had lifted up silly, sophomoric, and juvenile arguments to justify why he didn't believe. With all of the humility I can muster, I have to tell you that I devastated his arguments; I ate his lunch. And he knew it. He was reduced to speechlessness.

I expected, given the fact that he couldn't win the argument, that he would receive Christ. But he didn't. It was then that I realized he didn't believe because he didn't want to believe, not because he had good reasons to disbelieve.

Unbelief is hardly ever the result of reasoned and thoughtful arguments against belief. Unbelief is always a volitional choice most often secured by irrational or nonrational forces. In other words, you decide to disbelieve or not, reasons or no reasons or in spite of reason.

It's also true that belief requires a decision of the will, not just of the mind. And although there are good reasons for belief, one doesn't need reasons in order to believe. As Augustine said, "The world says seeing is believing. The Christian knows that believing is seeing." And believing is always ultimately a choice, reasons or no reasons but never in spite of reason.

TIME TO DRAW AWAY
❖

Read John 20:19-31, Romans 1:18-22.

For meditation:

*Is there anything about the faith that you find it difficult
to believe? If so, why? What are your reasons—
or non-reasons? If your disbelief is emotional,
psychological, or just plain stubborn, admit that.
Deal with it. Then choose to believe.*

On the other hand, if your disbelief has some apparent
rational justification, then explore the issues involved,
checking out the evidence for and against your disbelief.
God isn't threatened by rational inquiry. You see,
God is the God of our minds, not just of our hearts and
souls and bodies. He even calls skeptics to come and
reason with Him (Isaiah 1:18). So go ahead, investigate.
In the end, I think you'll come to see things His way anyway.

Facing Failure

My friend Fred Smith was once approached by a businessman who had run a multi-million dollar business into the ground. Many people had lost their jobs, and there had been great financial loss to the investors.

This man said to Fred, "I don't know what God is trying to teach me."

Amazed but calm, Fred said, "God is teaching you that you have made some stupid decisions."

Fred says that pagans blame failure on luck and Christians blame it on God, but in the end there isn't much difference. Failure is failure, and sometimes God allows it.

But let me tell you something you ought to remember: God has no vested interest in the failure of His people. He would honor you that you might honor Him. Nevertheless, the Christian who ignores good business practices (or good relational dynamics or good educational philosophy or good church management), thinking God will clean up his or her mess, is in for a rude awakening. "Do not be deceived: God cannot be mocked. A man reaps what he sows" (Galatians 6:7).

TIME TO DRAW AWAY
— ❖ —
Read Proverbs 10:4, 12:11, 14:23, 16:3, 21:5, 22:29.

For meditation:

Are you in a mess right now? Has a business deal failed, a relationship gone sour, a disciplinary measure backfired? Whatever the failure, strive to learn from it. Figure out as best you can what went wrong and why. You may need to seek the counsel of others—people who can be more objective about the matter. Do whatever it takes

157

to learn what mistakes you made, what you can do to avoid them the next time, and what positive steps you can take to make wiser choices.

God is pleased when you learn from your failures. That's why He permits them.

The Scars of Life

In *Pilgrim's Progress*, Valiant for Truth is talking about what he had heard from Truth Tell about Christian's death. He says,

> It was told what welcome he had at all his Lord's lodgings, specially when he came to the gates of the celestial city; for there, said the man, he was received with the sound of trumpet by a company of the shining ones. He told it also how all the bells of the city did ring for joy and what golden garments he was clothed with.

Valiant for Truth was sustained through many trials with those words. And then it came his time to die. "I am going to my Father's," he said. "And I am getting there through great difficulty. Yet I'm not sorry for all the trouble I have been through to arrive where I am. My marks and my scars I carry with me, to be a witness that I have fought the Father's battles."

You may be hurting now, but remember: You aren't home yet. And when you finally arrive there, you will be glad for the scars.

TIME TO DRAW AWAY
— ❖ —
Read Job 5:18, Romans 5:1-5.

For meditation:

Has life scarred you? You're not alone, and like everyone else who has been wounded, you need the Healer to come to your aid. If you haven't taken your hurts to Him yet, do so now. He knows hurts will come to you, but He's on your side, always ready to begin the healing process.

159

Truisms

Let me give you a quiz. It has three questions.

1. What is your opinion of the multiplication table?
2. What do you think about the law of gravity?
3. How do you feel about the roundness of the earth?

Does this quiz seem silly to you? After all, what sense does it make to ask someone's opinion about the multiplication table or the law of gravity or the earth's roundness? Those are facts about which one doesn't express an opinion. They're true, and that's that.

You know, that's how I feel when people question the existence of God. I want to say, "Look, are you some kind of fruitcake?" That, of course, is the English translation of the psalmist's words, "The fool says in his heart, 'There is no God'" (Psalm 14:1).

The logical question regarding God is, What is He like? The question, Does He exist? is silly. Of course He does. The universe abounds with the evidence of His presence, and it's so great that unbelievers are without excuse for their disbelief (Romans 1:20).

"What, then, is God like?" you ask. Look into the face of Jesus, see what He does, hear what He says, put your fingers in His nail-scarred hands, watch the angels of heaven bow down in worship of Him and notice how the demons shudder and run before Him, listen to the testimonies of those who have been healed by Him . . . then you'll begin to understand what God is like. "The Word became flesh and made his dwelling among us. We have seen his glory, the glory of the One and Only, who came from the Father, full of grace and truth" (John 1:14). That's true, and that's that.

TIME TO DRAW AWAY
———— ✤ ————
Read John 1:1-18, 14:1-11.

160

For meditation:

Center your attention on what God is like by focusing on Jesus. After all, He made the invisible God visible to us. What do you see? Hear? Feel? Think? What is your idea of God like? Check your understanding against Jesus', and if you see any differences, change your view to fit His. Only His is fully true, and that's that.

Discontentment

Someone tells of a king who was discontented. In fact he was so anxious, he couldn't sleep, rest, or think. He called his wise men and asked them what he could do.

One very old and very wise man said, "Find a man in your kingdom who is content, then wear his shirt for a day and a night, and you will be content."

That sounded like a good idea to the king, so he ordered some of his servants to search for such a person.

Days blended into weeks before his servants returned. "Well," said the king, "did you find a contented man?"

"Yes, sire," his servants replied.

"Where is his shirt?" asked the king.

"Your majesty, he didn't have one."

Have you ever thought that if you had more stuff you would be more contented? I've thought that sometimes. Now I have more stuff than I have ever had, but the stuff hasn't brought contentment. That's why I've gone to Jesus. When I lose the stuff, I'll still have Him and the contentment He gives.

TIME TO DRAW AWAY
———— ❖ ————

Read Psalm 49, 1 Timothy 6:6-11.

For meditation:

Have you rested your satisfaction in stuff?
Do you think that a new car or a new stereo or new clothes
or any other material thing will bring you contentment?
It won't, you know. Only Jesus can do that. Why don't you
place your trust in Him to bring you real satisfaction?

162

Rewards

During the Great Depression, Babe Ruth held out on his baseball contract until he had received an $80,000 deal. A club official protested to Ruth, "Do you realize that you are going to be paid more than President Hoover got last year?"

"Yes," Ruth replied. "But I had a better year than he had."

Some people believe that if they're good, love God, and do right, they will be rich and healthy in this life. Well, sometimes they will and sometimes they won't. But in the next life, that's when that lifestyle will really pay off. As Queen Victoria said to the Archbishop of Canterbury: "My lord of Canterbury, just because God doesn't balance His accounts every Thursday, it doesn't mean that He won't balance His accounts in the end."

For some people, God's balanced books will lead to incredible rewards. But for others . . . well, let's just say that a lot of folks will be very surprised before the throne. Unless, of course, they have a good lawyer. And the best one I know is Jesus. He never loses a case because He's the only One the Judge will listen to.

Tell me, who's your lawyer?

TIME TO DRAW AWAY
——————— ❖ ———————
Read 1 Corinthians 3:7-15, Hebrews 7:23-27.

For meditation:

Do you ever wonder if living right in this life is worth it?
Sometimes, it doesn't seem like it, but that's because
our ultimate rewards are heavenly, not earthly. And if your
faith is in Jesus, Heaven is a reward you definitely won't
miss. Think about that. Then thank God for it.

163

Servanthood

During the American Revolution, a man in civilian clothes rode past a group of soldiers repairing a small defensive barrier. Their leader was shouting instructions at them but making no other attempt to help them. Asked why by the rider, the leader said with great dignity, "Sir, I'm a corporal!"

The stranger apologized, dismounted, and proceeded to help the exhausted soldiers. The job done, he turned to the corporal and said, "If you need some more help, son, call me." With that, the Commander-In-Chief, George Washington, remounted his horse and rode on.

Jesus said that the greatest would be the least and the leader would be the servant. We don't buy into that truth much. Perhaps that's why there aren't very many true leaders anymore. It wouldn't be a bad idea for our leaders to climb down off their podiums and provide some hands-on help. Once we got over the shock, I think we would listen to them when they returned to their podiums and gave a speech.

TIME TO DRAW AWAY
————— ✤ —————
Read Matthew 20:20-28; Hebrews 13:7,17.

For meditation:

Do you want to be a leader?
Then you'd better learn how to serve.
By the way, "How is your serve?"
If it needs some help, Jesus knows what to do.
No one serves better than He does.

Experience

I read a while back about a man who had not received a promotion he thought he deserved. Not only that, a younger man had been given the promotion. So this disgruntled employee went to his boss and complained: "I can't see how you can give that man the job. After all, I've been here faithfully serving this company for years. I have twenty years' experience."

Without blinking an eye, his boss looked straight at him and replied, "No, you haven't had twenty years' experience. You have had one year's experience. And you have repeated it twenty times."

I love to hear Christians tell about how they became Christians. But I always want to ask, "That's fine, but what has happened in your life lately?"

John Wesley asked the young men he was ordaining into the ministry, "Are you moving on to perfection?" In other words, are you running in circles, or are you growing in grace? That's a good question. What would be *your* answer?

TIME TO DRAW AWAY
—— ❖ ——
Read 1 Corinthians 3:1-4, Hebrews 5:11–6:3.

For meditation:

*How long have you been a Christian? What do you have
to show for it in terms of a changed life? Are you growing
up in the faith, pressing on to maturity? If not,
what are you waiting for?*

165

Standing with the Family

One time I attended an ecclesiastical meeting where a friend of mine talked about the need for people being introduced to the Savior so they could be saved. But in this particular meeting, salvation wasn't thought to be a proper topic for discussion. In fact, people laughed at my brother in Christ. I didn't laugh. But I didn't stand with my friend either. I simply kept quiet.

That night, in my shame, I prayed, "Father, from now on when people laugh at one of Your servants, they will laugh at two of us because I'll stand with my brother."

On another occasion, a different friend of mine told me in reference to a brother in Christ who had done something crazy, "I'll tell you privately what happened." You see, when they laugh at one of us, they laugh at the rest of us too.

TIME TO DRAW AWAY
———— ❖ ————
Read Jeremiah 20:7-12, Matthew 27:27-31.

For meditation:

*Throughout history, those who have stood for God have
been ridiculed. It hasn't made any difference who they
were: prophets, priests, kings, queens, apostles, deacons,
laymen, laywomen, the Savior Himself. If you stand with
Him, you're going to get some laughs, and it won't be very
funny. But be of good cheer and stand strong
with the family of faith. God will have the last laugh,
and we'll all be laughing with Him.*

166

PART · THREE

OVERCOMING SETBACKS

Most of us feel we progress in life by small increments. Three steps forward, two steps back is a good year. In my case, however, it's often three steps forward, five back. But that's only what it *seems* like on occasion . . . for a season . . . just a while.

As the Bible tells us, God is at work in all of this. His purposes and His perspective are always present, behind the scenes. We just don't always see Him at work. We lose sight of Him, we wallow in circumstances, we forget.

What's important in the midst of setbacks is that we not forget a very important lesson: God has made us to overcome: setbacks, our spiritual foe, unbelief, the world . . . whatever causes us to stumble backwards.

What's amazing about God's grace in all this is that He gives us not only the authority to overcome (Luke 10:19) but also the power (Acts 1:8). Like a torrential downpour, the Spirit drenches us with power from above, but mostly we just lay there like wet dish rags on a kitchen counter. We could take advantage of His gift and accomplish great things in His name. Instead, we wallow in those circumstances and excuse our own unbelief. Still, God forgives and accepts and empowers, in spite of our unwillingness, our lack of courage, our fears, our pain. Because of Him, we can overcome.

Jim, a businessman in his mid-forties, was deeply immersed in his problems. His children were rebellious. His marriage to Lilly was on the brink of divorce. And although he was a financial success and had more money than he'd ever need, he was bored. His business had gone downhill, but all he had to do was take semi-retirement and he could spend his days playing tennis or looking for side business deals or buying new adult "toys." But he was still miserable. Somehow, he had lost the challenge and meaning of his work and his faith.

Then, one day at a Bible study, he listened intently as the teacher challenged the men to servanthood. Thinking he'd take the teacher seriously, he volunteered for a short-term mission trip to an Eastern European country.

He went. He's never been the same since. In one short reality check, Jim's life had been transformed. He came face to face with real needs. He'd been self-absorbed, like so many of us, for so long he'd forgotten what regular folks were like. He'd forgotten that people are more important to God than America's scorecard—the big bucks. He'd forgotten that being a servant requires that you get your hands dirty.

On that mission trip, he met a young Rumanian woman who had lost her parents to the Ceaucescu terrorists. He befriended her and discovered a woman with a vibrant faith, who still loved and served people despite her loss, despite her pain, despite her having been abused. He asked her why.

Standing on a war-torn street corner, she pointed down the block to an old, bomb-damaged church. As she looked at the cross atop the church's steeple, she began to weep. Through the tears and in broken English, she explained:

> No sacrifice I could ever make could do more than what Jesus has done for me. No problem I could ever have could be greater than what He endured for me. And nothing I could ever do could bring my parents back. But because Jesus overcame death, I'll see my parents again. Because Jesus overcame sin, I'll see God in the heavens. Because Jesus overcame the poisons of this world, I'm able to love my enemies.

This hard-headed businessman began to weep. He could not relate to the young woman's loss or to her war-ravaged past or to the poverty, squalor, and injustice she had endured. But he could connect with the poisons of this world. Gaining some self-control, Jim asked this young woman to pray for him as he returned to America. One simple prayer: "Lord, make me a servant, that I may draw upon Your power to overcome the world."

When Jim returned to the States, he related the story to his Bible study teacher, who months before had strongly counseled him against divorce. After hearing Jim's account, the teacher issued him a challenge: "Jim, be a servant to your wife for the next six months. If you don't see any changes, I'll change my tune about the divorce."

But Jim quickly answered: "No, that won't be necessary. Besides, I'd know your heart wouldn't be in such counsel. But I will take you up on the first part—I'll be her servant."

About four months later, Jim and the teacher were talking again. Jim told him that his family situation was showing some signs of surviving, even thriving a bit.

"Why?" the teacher asked.

"Because," Jim answered, "Jesus can overcome even a stubborn fool like myself. It just took a sweet little Rumanian girl to teach me. The joke is, I thought if I served Lilly for a long time, she'd really change. The truth is, I'm the one who's changed! I just can't believe what a difference it makes when your focus is on Jesus and others first instead of on yourself."

Perhaps your marriage is fine and your kids aren't rebellious and you're still excited about your work, but you have other big setbacks. Remember, you've been given authority and power to overcome: the enemy, unbelief, the world. You can do it. Jesus promises.

CHAPTER FIVE

REMINDERS
OF THE ALMIGHTY

✥

You, man of God, . . . pursue righteousness,
godliness, faith, love, endurance and gentleness.
Fight the good fight of the faith. Take hold of the
eternal life to which you were called when you
made your good confession in the presence of many
witnesses. In the sight of God, who gives life to
everything, and of Christ Jesus, who while testifying
before Pontius Pilate made the good confession,
I charge you to keep this command without spot or
blame until the appearing of our Lord Jesus Christ,
which God will bring about in his own time—God,
the blessed and only Ruler, the King of kings and
Lord of lords, who alone is immortal and who lives
in unapproachable light, whom no one has seen or
can see. To him be honor and might forever. Amen.

Paul the apostle
1 Timothy 6:11-16

God's Holiness

Do you know what irritates me? People who think they have God in their back pockets. God is not "the Man upstairs," nor is He, as a movie star put it, "a living doll." God is God.

> "For my thoughts are not your thoughts,
>   neither are your ways my ways," declares the LORD.
> "As the heavens are higher than the earth,
>   so are my ways higher than your ways
>   and my thoughts than your thoughts." (Isaiah 55:8-9)

F. W. Faber, author of *The Creator and the Creature*, put it this way:

We must wait for God, long, meekly, in the wind and wet, in the thunder and lightning, in the cold and dark. Wait, and He will come. He never comes to those who do not wait. When He comes, go with Him, but go slowly. Fall a little behind; when He quickens His pace, be sure of it, before you quicken yours. But when He slackens, slacken at once and do not be slow only . . . but silent, very silent . . . for He is God.

TIME TO DRAW AWAY
— ❖ —

Read Exodus 19:1-25, 20:18-21; Hebrews 12:18-29.

For meditation:

When you come before God in prayer or public worship, or when you speak about Him to others, do you do so with reverence and awe? Do you ever come before God and stay silent, realizing that you're in the presence of the Almighty Creator, the One who holds all things

in existence every moment of every day,
the One who will one day judge every human being?
Think about that as you go before Him today,
and be thankful that He's your Father, that He's on your
side in Christ rather than against you.

Timing

One time I conducted a wedding ceremony where the timing got off with the preliminary question addressed to the groom. The question was:

Sam, wilt thou have this woman to be thy wedded wife, and wilt thou pledge thy troth to her, in all love and honor, in all duty and service in all faith and tenderness, to live with her, and cherish her, according to the ordinance of God, in the holy bond of marriage?

That was the question, but I almost didn't get a chance to ask it.

I said, "Sam, wilt thou have . . ." and he said, "I will."

"Sam," I replied, "you have to wait until I ask you the question." He said the right thing but at the wrong time.

The same kind of thing happens to many Christians. Timing is so important.

Take witnessing, for example. So often we try to shove through doors that haven't even been set ajar, much less opened to us. So I've found that a good prayer in evangelism is, "Lord, You open the door and I'll walk through it. By Your grace, I won't try to kick it down."

We Christians need to be more sensitive to timing.

TIME TO DRAW AWAY
— ❖ —

Read Joshua 6:1-21, Nehemiah 1:1–2:10.

For meditation:

Are you wondering how and when to approach someone about an issue that needs some resolution? Or are you trying to decide when would be the best time to share your

174

*faith with a friend or loved one? Or is there some other
matter that requires just the right timing?
Take the situation before the Lord and ask Him
to show you when to act.*

God's Rules

Someone gave me several great rules of diet. Let me give you some of them.

- If you eat something and no one sees you eat it, it has no calories.
- If you drink a diet soda with a candy bar, the calories in the candy bar are canceled out by the diet soda.
- When you eat with other people, calories don't count if you don't eat more than they do.
- Cookie pieces contain no calories; the process of breaking causes calorie leakage.

Don't you wish those were true?

You see, there are certain inviolate rules built into the universe, so I'm afraid that wishing for fewer calories won't make it so. The other rules of God are like that too. He doesn't have rules to make you unhappy. Just the opposite. His word is simply the way the world works. Someone has said, "You don't break the Ten Commandments. You break yourself against them."

We would find life more enjoyable if we stopped fighting against God's rules.

TIME TO DRAW AWAY
———— ✥ ————

Read Psalm 119.

For meditation:

Circle or underline all the benefits of God's Word and knowing and obeying it mentioned in Psalm 119. You'll begin to get a taste of all that awaits those who guide their lives by God's loving counsel.

176

Incarnation

In one of the *Chronicles of Narnia, The Horse and His Boy,* by C. S. Lewis, there's a little girl by the name of Aravis who has a slave girl. She treats her slave horribly. Aslan, the Christ-figure in the *Chronicles* series, comes to Aravis and scratches her. She asks why he did it, and Aslan answers, "I didn't scratch you because you need to be punished. I scratched you because you needed to know what it feels like."

That's what Christ did. He entered time and space, He walked our dirty roads, and He died in our place. He learned firsthand what it feels like to be in a fallen world. Jesus entered time and space, not just to keep you from being lonely or afraid but to be lonely and afraid. Not just to keep you from dying but to die. Because He knows what it feels like, the Bible says, He is kind and gentle.

Go to Him. He longs to show you what unconditional love feels like.

TIME TO DRAW AWAY
———— ❖ ————

Read John 19:1-30, Hebrews 2:9-18.

For meditation:

Regardless of what you're going through,
Christ understands and desires with His whole being
to shower you with His love, His mercy, His grace.
Don't wait another second. Turn to Him now.
He's eagerly waiting.

Christmas Is About Love

As you may know, Christmas has not been my favorite time of the year in the past. I suspect my dislike of Christmas had something to do with the fact that, for almost thirty years, I had been a pastor.

If you're a pastor, the Christmas season can really do some terrible things to your life. For instance, you must lead more worship services. That means more sermons and more preparation.

Furthermore, everybody is busy at Christmas, so the normal work of the church has to come to a screeching halt. Everybody is too busy to do anything except think about Christmas. And that puts a real dent in the availability of volunteer help for the church's ongoing work.

Also, for some reason, at Christmas the problems most people face are magnified. People who are lonely feel more lonely. People who don't feel accepted or affirmed feel even less so. Family problems have a way of becoming monster problems around Christmas time. Drunks get drunker, angry people become more angry, and fearful people become more fearful. That, in turn, increases the pastor's counseling load.

And then, if you're a pastor, you have to do all of the other stuff regular people have to do around Christmas. Things like shopping for presents, going to Christmas get-togethers, and all that kind of stuff.

By the time Christmas is over, most pastors are ready for a rest in the psychiatric ward of the local hospital. The nervous breakdown is well deserved. After all, the pastor worked hard for it, and he deserves it.

But this Christmas, I'm not a pastor. To be perfectly honest with you, it feels a little funny. Instead of thinking about how busy I am, I'm thinking about how loving God was. Instead of thinking about the Christmas sermons and how to deal with old themes in a new way, I'm thinking about the sermon He preached in a stable in Bethlehem. Instead of having a pity party, I'm having a birthday party. It isn't my birthday, but it is His Son's. And so, for the first time in a long time, I've been able to be still a little bit and think about what Christmas really means.

Christmas is about a lot of nice things. Christmas is about the worship of a God who would enter time and space. Christmas is about friends and family. Christmas is about giving and caring. It's about rejoicing because one is a part of the family of God. It's about truth and salvation. But mostly, Christmas is about love—a love so incredible and so wonderful that it almost defies our ability to believe it.

"For God so loved the world . . ." That is a good statement, and a comforting one if you can believe it. But it could also be the naiveté of wish fulfillment. It could be nothing more than a positive platitude or a religious slogan. After all, if God loves the world, how come there are so many problems? If God loves the world, how come I hurt so much?

She was fifteen and he was seventeen when they met. All through high school, they went steady. So after high school, no one was surprised when they got married.

Some four years and two children later, she was standing in her kitchen with a pile of dirty dishes in the sink and a pile of dirty diapers in the corner. Tears were streaming down her face. Looking back, she could never be quite sure why she made the decision, but she did make it. She took off her apron and walked out.

She called that night and her young husband answered the phone. He was understandably quite worried and also quite angry.

"Where are you?!" he demanded, his concern and his anger fighting for control of his voice.

"How are the children?" she asked, ignoring his question.

"Well, if you mean to ask if they are fed, they are. I've also put them to bed. They are wondering, just as I am, what you think you are doing."

She hung up that night, but it wasn't the last of the phone calls. In fact, she called almost every week for the next three months. Her husband, knowing that something was seriously wrong, began, in those phone calls, to plead with her to come home. He would tell her that the children were with their grandparents during the day and were well cared for. But he would also tell her that he loved her. He would tell her how much they all missed her, and then he would try to find out where she was. Whenever the conversation turned to her whereabouts, she would hang up.

Finally, the young husband could stand it no longer. He took their savings and hired a private detective to find his wife. The detective

179

found her and reported that she was in a third-rate hotel across the country in Des Moines, Iowa.

The young man borrowed some money from his in-laws, bought a plane ticket, and flew to Des Moines. After taking a cab from the airport to the hotel, he climbed the stairs to his wife's third-floor room. (Those kinds of hotels don't have elevators.) If you had been there, you would have seen the doubt in his eyes and the perspiration on his forehead. His hand trembled as he knocked on the door.

When his wife opened the door, he forgot his prepared speech and simply said, "We love you so much. Won't you come home?"

She fell apart in his arms. They went home together.

One evening, some weeks later, the children were in bed, and he and his wife were sitting in the living room before the fire. He finally got up enough courage to ask the question that had haunted him for so many months: "Why wouldn't you come home? Why, when I told you over and over again that I loved you and missed you, didn't you come home?"

"Because," she said with profound simplicity, "before those were only words. *But then you came.*"

It's nice to think that God loved the world. But, at the first Christmas, He didn't tell us in just words, nor did He use platitudes or cliches. He came. In His Son, He came.

When Disraeli married Mary Lewis, she was twelve years his senior. While Disraeli was certainly not destitute, Mary Lewis was a wealthy woman. Their love for each other was legendary.

Sometimes Disraeli and Mary would kid each other about their marriage. Disraeli would say, "Mary, I only married you for your money."

"Yes," Mary would reply, "but dear, if you had it to do over again, you would do it for love."

Most of us came to Christ for a variety of reasons. Some of us were without meaning in our lives. Others of us were overwhelmed about our sin and guilt. Perhaps there was a particular problem that drove us to Christ. Maybe we simply felt that the gospel made sense and accepted Christ in the same way one accepts the multiplication table. But, after walking with Him, all of us could say with Mary Lewis, "If we had it to do over again, it would be for love."

I've been thinking about Christmas this year. It's the first time in quite a while that I've been able to give it much thought. I've decided that it is about love. It's the time when God, who had no reason to love us, demonstrated His love in an incredible way: He came. Into our world in a way we could unfailingly see, He came.

TIME TO DRAW AWAY
———— ✢ ————

Read Luke 2:1-38, John 3:16-18.

For meditation:

Think of someone who has loved you, who has shown any kind of concern or care or interest in you for your own sake. Now purge that love of any tinge of selfishness, couple it to everything good, and multiply its expression by infinity. That's what God's love for you is really like. Incredible? Infinitely so! That's why He had to give us some tangible expression of His unfathomable love. That's the Incarnation, that's Christmas, that's Christ.

181

Searching for God

Let me give you a principle that is a very important one if you are searching for God. The principle is this: *God will take seriously your search for Him to the exact same degree to which you seriously search for Him.* That's true for Christians and nonChristians too. Once we get serious, He gets serious too.

Did you hear about the archbishop who went to the cathedral for his evening devotions? He knelt down at the foot of the chancel steps and prayed, "Oh, God . . ." A voice said, "Yes, what is it?"

They found the archbishop the next morning. He had died of a coronary.

What would you do if God really answered you? What if He said something you didn't like? Maybe you don't want Him to answer—and maybe that's the reason He hasn't.

God will take seriously your search for Him to the exact same degree to which you seriously search for Him. How serious are you?

TIME TO DRAW AWAY
❖

Read 1 Samuel 1, Hebrews 11:6.

For meditation:

Do you want to know God's will for your life?
Do you really want to know God intimately? If so, how
serious are you in your search? Are you spending regular
time with Him? Are you diligently studying His Word?
Are you faithful in your worship of Him? Are you leaning
on Him, seeking to obey Him in the power of His Spirit?
He'll reward your search but only if it's an authentic,
persistent one. Is it?

Approval

I'm told that at the Pacific Ocean Studios on Clement Street in San Francisco, there is a pipe organ called the "Chamberlain Music Master." What's different about this pipe organ is that it has a special button, and when you push it, you get a round of applause of concert-hall size. So you can play anything, press the button, and get a virtual standing ovation.

When I heard about that, I thought, *That's exactly what most folks are working for—the applause of others. That's empty, meaningless, and silly.*

The only approval rating that's important is the one God gives you. The next time you have pleased everybody else, before you go to bed, kneel down and see if God is pleased. If He isn't, the pleasure you brought to others doesn't mean anything.

It's hard to perform for an audience that doesn't applaud, unless, of course, God is the One applauding. Can you hear Him clapping?

TIME TO DRAW AWAY
─────── ❖ ───────
Read Isaiah 58, Matthew 23.

For meditation:

Who are you living to please? Is God your audience, or are you performing for others? Whose applause do you value the most? Unless it's God's, your performance is doomed to a very bad review from the only Critic who really matters.

Best of Luck?

A pastor was leaving his pastorate, and some friends sent him flowers as a going-away gesture. But the florist got the flowers meant for the pastor mixed up with flowers that were supposed to go to a funeral.

The next day, the pastor was laughing with the florist. The pastor remarked, "I was wondering why there was a sympathy card in my flowers."

The florist said, "I'm not really worried about that. But the flowers I sent to the funeral had your card in them. And it read, 'Best of luck in your new location.'"

Dear friend, Heaven doesn't have a thing to do with luck. It has to do with a promise made by the only Man who was ever there and came back to talk about it. He said, "I am going there to prepare a place for you. . . . I will come back and take you to be with me" (John 14:2-3). His name is Jesus, and He never gets His cards mixed up. If you know Him, He has a new location waiting for you.

TIME TO DRAW AWAY
❖

Read Luke 23:39-43, Romans 8:28-39.

For meditation:

*If you belong to Christ, Heaven is your home—guaranteed,
no exceptions. Nothing can separate you from Him—
not one single thing.*

*Place your trust in Him, then rest in His ability to save you
for Paradise. Certainly the Creator and Sustainer of the
entire universe can handle getting you to Heaven,
don't you think?*

When God Says, "It's Enough!"

Have you ever met anyone who liked to go to the dentist? My dentist friends have told me that their profession takes an incredible toll on their fellow practitioners because it's a thankless job. If your surgeon hurts you terribly, once you're out of the operating room, you thank him or her profusely. If your pastor comes and offers a prayer, he is thanked for offering it. But a dentist is hardly ever thanked. In fact, most folks are in such a hurry to get out of the dental office that all you usually see are heels and elbows.

There is, however, one really nice thing about going to the dentist. It's that time toward the end of your visit when the drill stops and the dentist looks into your mouth and utters those glorious words: "It's enough. That's about it. Rinse your mouth out." To me, when the dentist says that, it's almost as good as the time when Jesus will say, "Well done, good and faithful servant!" (Matthew 25:21).

God sometimes echoes something similar to what one hears from the dentist. You go through a horrible time in your life and you wonder if it is ever going to end, and then, for no explainable reason, everything changes—things start looking up, the depression lifts, the situation changes and, all of a sudden, you can see the Son shine again. That's when you know God has said, "It's enough. That's about it."

A dear friend has been an encouragement to me and our entire staff at Key Life from the first days of our ministry. I've never met her, but I love her a lot.

Our friend was in the coffee business and, just when Key Life Network was starting, she gave Key Life an electric coffee maker. Sometimes, when we were struggling, we would receive a shipment of coffee from her. At other times in those early days (it still happens occasionally), we would get worried about whether or not we were going to make it and she would call or write and say, "The Lord has called you into this, and He is going to honor it. You keep on keeping on. I'm praying for you." One would have thought that she didn't have a care in the world. But if you had read her letters of encouragement or listened to her "up" phone conversations and had thought that, you would have been wrong.

Over the past five years she has gone through more troubled waters than Job. She has had some serious physical problems, and on two or three occasions, she came very near death. A major fire broke out in her home, and it almost wiped her out. She has faced some incredible emotional stress stemming from a variety of areas, and her financial problems have, at times, been nothing less than desperate. She has faced the death of some people she loved very much, some unjustified criticism from people she thought loved her, and, on occasion, a total inability to work to earn a living. And yet, during all that time she was encouraging us!

But not only through her words. By persevering through all that pain, she inspired us. In those early days of Key Life when we honestly felt we might not make it as a viable ministry, our staff often prayed for her and figured that if she could hang tough, we could too.

I got a letter this morning from our friend. Let me quote from part of it.

Just received your newsletter and wanted you to know that I am grateful to say that after five years of walking in dark valleys of bad health, financial problems and emotional stress, God has seen fit to drive away the dark clouds from my sky and place me on a beautiful spot atop a mountain where I can see where I've been and why.

She went on to explain the reversal of her financial situation, God's miraculous physical intervention in her health problems, and the resolution of a number of areas in her life where she had been under extreme pressure. God had finally told her, "It's enough."

Why did God change her situation? Don't ask me; I don't know why. The Lord hardly ever checks with me about anything. Besides, as C. S. Lewis had Aslan the lion say to the children, I'm "not given to know anybody's story" but my own, and sometimes I'm not even sure about that one.

Nevertheless, without explanation or warning or fanfare, everything changed from bad to good. God had decided that it was enough. Her loving heavenly Father determined that, for whatever reason, it was time for the period of hardship, testing, and pain to come to an end.

That was the experience of Job too. When Job first started experiencing the devastation of everything important in his life, he was quite spiritual about the matter. He said with great faith and submission, "Shall we accept good from God and not trouble?" (Job 2:10). The one recording all this commented, "In all this, Job did not sin in what he said." Job must have thought, *Certainly things can't get any worse.* But they did. When his hardship and pain went from bad to really bad, the clichés and the platitudes melted away. It's interesting to watch the gradual loss of easy spirituality in Job's life. He even finally reached the place where all he wanted to do was die.

However, the most difficult thing Job faced was that he didn't know why all of these bad things were happening to him. (We, of course, are allowed to see what was going on behind the scenes in Job 1 and 2, but Job didn't get a chance to read those chapters.) So Job sets his case before God, calling on Him to vindicate him. But when God shows up and runs a rather long series of questions past Job designed to humble him, he says "Oops!" then God really steps in: "The LORD made him prosperous again and gave him twice as much as he had before" (42:10). In other words, God said, "It's enough."

You may be going through a divorce or facing very difficult physical problems or feeling debilitated by guilt or experiencing incredible family problems. Maybe your finances are a hassle, you're suffering the loneliness of lost friendships or the death of a loved one. Perhaps you're dealing with a past filled with the trauma of abuse and abandonment. Or maybe you're worried about your children or your parents. You know the Bible says that "in all things God works for the good of those who love him" (Romans 8:28), but when the pain is horrible and the fear so real you can hardly stand it, you may have a tendency to wonder.

I'm not a guru, and I certainly don't know all the reasons any of us has to go through difficult times. Sure, there are some biblical answers to the questions asked in the pain. There are doctrinal and theological ways to resolve one's intellectual dilemmas. Sometimes God is teaching us things we need to learn. There are times when God in His sovereign love chooses to reveal to us why we have to face the pain. But sometimes Heaven seems cold and silent. I know. I've experienced that too. The fact is, much of the bad stuff we have to face now we won't understand until we get home. In the meantime, I've got some good news for you.

First, God loves you and He doesn't do anything without reason. There's meaning and wisdom behind your pain, even if you don't see it. Peter wrote, "Dear friends, do not be surprised at the painful trial you are suffering, as though something strange were happening to you. But rejoice that you participate in the sufferings of Christ, so that you may be overjoyed when his glory is revealed" (1 Peter 4:12-13).

And second, God knows you and what you can bear. He will accomplish His purpose, and then, when His purpose is accomplished, He will say like the dentist: "That's about it. It's enough." He will say that at exactly the right time—and that time may be very soon.

My brother, Ron, lived with Anna and me one of the summers he was in law school. During that summer, he started working as a waiter in an exclusive Cape Cod restaurant. My brother was a wonderful law student, but he wasn't a great waiter. In fact, he was fired after only two days on the job. He really needed the job to earn some money for his educational expenses, and I expected his dismissal would have devastated him. I remember going out into the backyard to comfort him only to find that he wasn't depressed at all. In fact, he was in very good spirits. When I asked him why, he said, "Steve, I've been thinking about it, and I decided that I didn't need to be depressed because the next minute may change my life."

He was right, you know. The next minute may change your life. It's great when God and dentists say, "That's about it. It's enough."

TIME TO DRAW AWAY

———— ❖ ————

Read Daniel 4:28-37, John 9:1-7.

For meditation:

Do you feel stretched to the limit? Is the pain,
the confusion, the struggle almost more than you can bear?
God will not desert you; He will not let you languish
without hope, without help. Sometimes it seems He will,
I know. But the time will come when He says,
"It's enough," and your hardship will pass away.

Until then, stay close to Him, drawing
on His infinite resources.

CHAPTER SIX

CREATIVE BEHAVIOR THAT OVERCOMES

*Do not repay anyone evil for evil. Be careful to do
what is right in the eyes of everybody.
If it is possible, as far as it depends on you,
live at peace with everyone. Do not take revenge,
my friends, but leave room for God's wrath, for it is
written: "It is mine to avenge; I will repay," says
the Lord. On the contrary:
"If your enemy is hungry, feed him;
if he is thirsty, give him something to drink.
In doing this, you will heap burning
coals on his head."
Do not be overcome by evil,
but overcome evil with good.*

Paul the apostle
Romans 12:17-21

Daring to Doubt

Do you have doubts about the faith? "No," you say, "I've been a Christian for years." You don't understand. I didn't ask if you were a Christian or not. I asked if you had some doubts, perhaps a nagging question in the back of your mind, "Is this stuff really true?" It's okay to ask that question, even if you're already a Christian.

For both the doubting Christian and the searching skeptic, we're going to look at some prerequisites for faith—conditions you must fulfill when you have doubts—as seen in the life of "doubting Thomas." The question at hand is, What was it about Thomas that caused Jesus to deal with his doubts? Let's find out. First read the account about Thomas and his doubts in John 20:24-31, then plunge into what follows below.

When you look at this disciple of Jesus, one of the first things you notice is that Thomas was a man who was willing to risk. You must remember that Thomas was not a mere dabbler in religion. He was a Christ-follower, and he was committed to following Him to the death. He was willing to risk in order to discover. If you aren't willing to risk, forget it.

Socrates, Plato's mentor, had a student who came to him while he was kneeling by a stream. The student asked Socrates, "What is truth?" Without hesitation, Socrates grabbed the boy, held him under water until the boy began to struggle, pulled him up, and answered, "When you want knowledge the way you just wanted air, then you shall have it."

If you don't believe something and your disbelief doesn't bother you, then forget about resolving your doubts. You don't want answers badly enough yet.

Thomas was also a man who refused to run on someone else's gasoline. If we had been around when the disciples said they had seen the risen Jesus, many of us would have said, "Oh, really? What a fantastic experience. Can I vicariously share it with you?" But, you see, you can't vicariously share anyone else's belief or experience.

190

Fred Smith once told me that when he first became a Christian, he had serious doubts. When I asked him how he dealt with them, he said that he believed because his friend Howard Butt believed. "Sometimes," Fred told me, "Howard would be off talking to the Lord, and I would look at him and think, 'I can't believe, but he does, and I believe because he does.'"

That kind of belief is okay for a transition period between unbelief and belief, but you can't travel long on that kind of fuel. To try would be like telling your wife, "Honey, I've got a backache. Would you take an aspirin?" It may help you see that an aspirin is easy to swallow, but it will do nothing for your backache. In order to resolve doubt, you need to decide that you will seek God yourself.

I know a man who became a Christian a number of years ago. What led up to his conversion illustrates my point. One day he went to his backyard, his Bible in tow, and looking up to the sky, said, "Lord, I'm not trying to put You to the test, but if You don't speak to me, I'm going to take this Bible and throw it away." Now that's not an appropriate way to go before God, but his heart was right. He was saying, "I've been playing a game. I've been running on the gasoline of others. Now I have to meet You or I'm going to die."

Turning back to Thomas, we can also see that he was a man of questions. I saw an advertisement that read: "The only dumb questions are the ones that aren't asked." God would say that too. Questions that concern your doubts do have answers, but when they aren't asked, you won't find the answers. Will Rogers once said that he believed in college because it took kids away from home just at the point when they started asking questions. There might be something to that. But if the home or the church can't be open enough to any question that anyone asks, then we have a serious problem. Thomas was a man of questions. That's why he got some answers.

Furthermore, Thomas verbalized his doubts. One of the problems with the church is that when we are hurting—and doubt is one of the greatest hurts we can have—many of us play pretend. We keep quiet about it, never getting our needs met. That's like going to the doctor because you have stomach pains and when the doctor asks you, "Where does it hurt?" you say, "I'm not going to tell you because you will think I'm sick." How foolish! How foolish for those of us in the church who do the same thing.

If you have doubts, don't go off in a corner and lick your wounds. Be like Thomas: Verbalize your doubts, and let the church come to your side with some answers.

Finally, Thomas was a man who, when he found answers, was willing to accept them and act on them.

Have you ever met a person who likes to travel but doesn't care if he gets anywhere? Calvin, a German shepherd we once had, was like that. You would just jingle his chain and he would get all excited, knowing he was going to get to ride in the car. Sometimes the ride would lead to swimming, while other times it led to the vet and a shot. Calvin didn't care. Where he was going wasn't important; that he was going was.

Many Christians are like that. They verbalize their doubts just to get sympathy, not because they plan to do anything about them even if they ever got answers. But the reason for speaking up about your doubts is to get satisfactory answers that lead somewhere—to a changed life. You ask questions, not to show how deep your philosophical nature is, but to get answers. The reasons you risk should have nothing to do with showing your courage, but they should have everything to do with finding the reality of God.

Jesus answered Thomas' doubts exactly, precisely, and totally. And Thomas didn't even know Jesus had heard the question. Jesus met his doubts in two ways.

First, Jesus gave him an evidential answer: He showed Thomas His wounds and allowed Thomas to check them out himself. If you believe there's no evidence for the truth of the Christian faith, then you believe a lie. The Christian faith is credible, evidential, it hangs together, and it is totally open to questioning.

One reason so many believers have such terrible doubts is that they're afraid Christianity may not be true. So they don't probe and find out. They would rather hang on to what may be false rather than risk to confirm that it's really true. If that's you, I've got some good news for you. Christianity is true. It's factually, actually, really true. Go ahead. Check it out. Truth never fears investigation.

A pastor said that one day he was sitting at his desk when he heard a cry concerning his grandson, John: "John has fallen in the well, and he is dead! John is dead!" The pastor jumped from his desk and ran as fast as he could to the well. When he got there, he peered down and called out, "John, are you dead?"

A voice came up from the bottom of the well, "Yes, Grandfather, I'm dead."

The pastor replied, "Well, I am glad to hear it from your lips."

God isn't dead. He still speaks in the evidence He has so graciously given us. When you waver in your faith, it's often because you doubt. If you doubt, it may be because you simply haven't looked down into the well of truth.

The answer Jesus gave was not only evidential but also existential. He didn't just give the facts; He gave Himself too. That is the magnificent fact of Christian apologetics. The evidence is there, but the One about whom the evidence speaks is also there.

I heard that C. S. Lewis said that every time he sat down to write, he felt someone standing behind him watching. He described the experience this way: "To say that I was searching for God was like saying that a mouse was searching for a cat." Jesus comes, the evidence is presented, and then He says to both the shaking believer and the confirmed atheist, "Consider the evidence, but don't forget that I'm here also."

God doesn't play games. He's in the business of answering honest questions, meeting honest doubts, honoring genuine risk. When you go to the Father, expect answers to your questions, but if you don't really want to know, don't ask.

TIME TO DRAW AWAY
—————— ❖ ——————

Read 1 Kings 18:20-45, John 20:30-31.

For meditation:

What doubts do you have about the Christian faith? Write them down, then begin to search for answers. Hook up with some Christians who won't be threatened by your search. Let them guide you to some good sources of information. Whatever you do, don't let your doubts go unaddressed. You might not always find answers, but as you find more and more answers to your doubts, those that remain without answers will not seem so impossible to resolve, and they certainly won't be stumbling blocks to your faith anymore.

193

Concrete, Creativity, and the Creator

When I got off the airplane on my way to a speaking engagement at a church in the inner city, I was picked up in a limousine and driven to the church through some of the worst slums you can imagine. When we got to the church, which was surrounded by a high concrete wall, a gate was opened and I was ushered to the front door. The people at the dinner were all white, middle-class, and elderly.

Before I spoke, a number of people asked me what they could do about their dying church. One woman said, "Our problem is that we are not attracting young people. Mr. Brown, what can we do?"

I responded by telling her, and all those who were within earshot, that the first thing they should do is get a bulldozer and destroy the concrete wall surrounding their church. That way they wouldn't be insulated from the people Jesus wanted to reach.

Jesus said that "the gates of Hades" would not prevail against the church (Matthew 16:18). I don't know about you, but I always thought that passage was teaching that the church would have strong gates and that because of that it would stand no matter what. I thought that until I heard a preacher ask a very important question: "Have you ever been attacked by a gate?" That's a good question, and it points to an insightful fact: We don't have to protect anything. God is God, and He is quite capable of protecting what He wants to. We, on the other hand, are to be open and aggressive, knowing that we operate under the authority of Christ. We are not called to protect gates; we are called to attack them.

One of the problems we face as Christians is that many of us have developed a "protectionist" mentality about our relationship to the world. We build our fortresses and spend all of our time manning the walls lest the enemy should catch us unawares. But nothing could be further from the biblical view. The world's gates are to be attacked, and our walls are to be torn down.

Nowhere is the problem of walls more apparent than in the contemporary church's relationship to the arts. If a painting isn't "The

194

Praying Hands," Solomon's "Head of Christ," or Leonardo da Vinci's "The Last Supper," it can't seem to find a place in the church. Music, too, is carefully dichotomized between secular and sacred. The latter is appropriate for the church, while the former is for nightclubs and bars, but God forbid that the secular and sacred forms should ever mix. Or take drama. Drama is okay as long as the shepherds wear bathrobes and the story told is found in the Bible.

Did you know that the arts in Western civilization find their roots in the church? Did you know that those artists who were creative, innovative, and gifted found a haven of welcome among the people of God? Did you know that the natural place for the arts is the church? What happened? What went wrong between those times and ours? Let me tell you: We built a wall and tried to protect ourselves. In so doing, we robbed ourselves of the legitimate gift of beauty, and we robbed those who are creative of their legitimate home. Principle Forsyth, writing in the book *Christ and the Fine Arts*, states:

The principle of art is the incarnation of God's eternal beauty; the principle of the Christian faith is the incarnation of God's eternal human heart. Neither can do the other's work, yet their work is complimentary, and I wish the divorce between them—art and Christianity—were more nearly healed. I wish the artists felt more of the need which art can never fill; and I wish the Christians felt more of the need that art alone can fill.

It is important that the creative Christians who have gifts in the arts are welcomed into our churches and given opportunities to express "the creative gift" from God. That gift, as with all of God's gifts, should be received by God's church with joy and thanksgiving. After all, "The earth is the LORD's and everything in it, the world, and all who live in it" (Psalm 24:1). When the arts bring beauty, truth, and integrity to any subject or project, they are a part of God's creation and they bring honor to God's name.

Art isn't propaganda. It's worship. When we build a wall between the so-called sacred and secular and the wall is not commanded or ordained by God, we hurt people on both sides of the wall.

We don't have to worry about protecting our faith. You don't have to protect a lion; you just let him loose and he takes care of the rest.

What we need is to get a bulldozer and tear down the walls God didn't create and build bridges in their place.

TIME TO DRAW AWAY
—————— ❖ ——————

Read Psalm 150, 1 Corinthians 5:9-10, Titus 1:15-16.

For meditation:

Are you a bridge builder or a wall constructor? Are you trying to separate yourself from the world by shutting the world out, or are you striving to stay unstained by the world while reaching out to it in love, mercy, and grace?

God wants builders, and He sent us His Son so we could see the master Builder at work. Christ certainly never constructed walls between Himself and the world. If anything, He spent so much time building bridges to the world that He got the reputation of being a drunk, glutton, and friend of tax collectors and sinners (Matthew 11:19).

Does the world see enough in your life to slap the same reputation on you? God certainly hopes so.

The Mustard Seed Conspiracy

The Christian faith isn't something superficial and shallow. It's a whole new way of life that can only be described as a new birth or a new creation. To the Corinthian church, Paul said, "If anyone is in Christ, he is a new creation; the old has gone, the new has come!" (2 Corinthians 5:17).

Given this, we can see that the acting principle is: *In the business of spiritual reproduction, we reproduce after our own kind, just as we do in the realm of the physical.* If we're immature Christians, we're going to see more immature Christians in the church. If we're shallow and superficial, we're going to see more shallow and superficial Christians in the church. But if we're walking in the Spirit, we'll see others walk in the Spirit also. If we're growing in grace, we'll see others grow in grace. We reproduce after our own kind.

Since that's the case, how do we become mature in Christ? What does Christian maturity mean, anyway? In Ephesians 4:11-16, the Apostle Paul defines maturity in four ways, and each one helps us see how we can really grow up in Christ.

First, notice that Paul, speaking for God and undergirded by the Holy Spirit, defines maturity in terms of knowledge. You can't grow until you know.

The first church I ever served was on Cape Cod. I had a great time the first three years because I had never read the Bible intelligently. Nobody ever told me what a pastor was supposed to do, so I reviewed books from the pulpit on Sunday morning. By Wednesday, I had finished everything I was supposed to do in that little church, so I went out and played golf and fished the rest of the week. I thought, *Everybody talks about how hard it is to be a pastor. I don't understand them. This is the most wonderful job I have ever found. I've got it made. It's just like a vacation.*

Then, all of a sudden, I began to know and I began to grow. I began to find out that being a pastor meant letting people in on the truth—truth

197

that I had to learn first. From that point on, my life changed. Once I knew, I had to grow.

Our "Operations Manual" is the Bible. If we're not consulting it daily, we're going to get lost. Have you seen the bumper sticker that says, "Don't follow me, I'm lost"? I don't know about you, but I have no sense of direction. The truth is, I stay lost most of the time. Likewise, Christians have been giving that impression to others because we often don't know where we're going. We would, though, if we were consulting God's Word daily. And that can be just plain hard work at times.

Coming to Christ is quite simple. It's a simple act of faith on our part; it's receiving a gift. However, if anybody told you that living the Christian faith is simple, somebody lied to you, because it's just not true.

Second, Paul defines maturity in terms of growth. In the Methodist church, before any minister is ordained, he is asked, "Are you moving on to perfection?" All Christians need to ask that of themselves.

One of the young Christians in a church I once served stood up and gave testimony as to what God was doing in his life. He said, "I've come back. A lot of you thought I was backsliding. I didn't backslide. I just stopped and the light went out."

God calls us to grow. Are you growing? I didn't ask if you were perfect. I didn't ask if you had stopped sinning. I asked if you're growing. Nobody will know whether you're growing or not except you and God because only you and He know where you started.

In Mark 4, Jesus teaches that the kingdom of God is within. He says the kingdom of God is "like a mustard seed, which is the smallest seed you plant in the ground. Yet when planted, it grows and becomes the largest of all garden plants, with such big branches that the birds of the air can perch in its shade" (verses 31-32). Is that seed growing in your life? Can you see a before and an after picture? If you look back five years, can you see change in your life? Are you allowing the Spirit of God to transform you?

Third, Paul defines maturity in terms of Christlikeness. Many Christians seem to spend much of their time comparing themselves with their brothers and sisters in the faith. We say to ourselves, "I couldn't possibly be so bad. I'm more obedient than they are. I know the Bible better than they do. I'm following and growing in grace better than they are." The Bible says that we're not to compare ourselves with other believers but only with Christ. When we compare ourselves to each other, we're shooting too low. Our sights need to be higher because, as Bernard of Clairvaux said, "We always grow to resemble that which we love."

At an annual dog show in my hometown, they gave a ribbon for the owner who looked the most like his or her dog. Year after year, one of the morning radio personalities who had bull dogs won that award. The newspaper would always snap a picture of the man with his head down beside one of his dog's heads. He and his dogs looked exactly alike, but I did hear his wife say one time, "He loves those dogs more than he loves me."

We grow to resemble that which we love. What are you growing to resemble? Christ? What is Christ like? Christ is a miracle looking for a place to happen. Christ loves changed people, and He's in the business of doing the changing.

Remember when Christ called Zacchaeus down from the tree and the most exciting dinner party took place? Zacchaeus gave up everything and followed Jesus Christ because Jesus loved him. Does your love cause a change in other people? Jesus took the time to listen, to understand, to find out where people were and where they were hurting. Do you do that? Are you growing? Are you moving on to perfection? Are you becoming like Him?

Fourth, Paul defines Christian maturity in terms of utter dependence. In Ephesians 5, Paul tells us that we're to be filled with the Holy Spirit. Let me put that simply: The Christian faith is no more and no less than allowing Christ to do in us what we can't do ourselves.

Jim, a friend of mine, flies a small plane, and I've flown with him several times. You need to know I'm afraid of flying. When I've admitted that, people have said, "Where is your faith?" My faith is used up when I get on an airplane.

To sit right next to Jim and watch him fly, to look at that confusing panel in front of him, not knowing what a single one of those gadgets does, means that I have to be utterly and totally dependent on my friend, the pilot. At times, I'm scared to death, but there's nothing I can do about it, because when you're up there, you can't jump (at least not without a parachute, and that I'd never do). You can't tell the pilot to slow down so you can climb out. So I watch Jim like a hawk. When he perspires, I get worried. When he feels good, I do too (but I still worry).

Flying with him has taught me a valuable lesson in dependence: God wants us to be in exactly the same place that I am with Jim in an airplane. I have to trust Jim that he knows what he's doing. I have to trust that he will get us to our destination. God wants to do that in your life and mine. He wants our utter dependence (John 15:5, Galatians 2:20).

In ancient times there lived a very wise tutor who was called upon to teach the son of a great king. The tutor had a terrible time with this prince. The young man was a difficult child. To be more accurate, the prince was a spoiled brat. The tutor tried everything to get him to grow, to come to maturity. He tried cajoling, pushing, and shoving. Nothing worked. Finally, the tutor got an idea. He cut a strip of royal purple and pinned it to the young man's coat. The prince said, "What are you doing that for?" The tutor answered, "Because every time you look at that strip of purple, you'll remember that you're the king's son and behave accordingly."

You are "a chosen people, a royal priesthood, a holy nation, a people belonging to God, that you may declare the praises of him who called you out of darkness into his marvelous light" (1 Peter 2:9). You're the King's son. You're the King's daughter. Remember that.

TIME TO DRAW AWAY
———— ❖ ————

Read Romans 8:1-17, Galatians 5:16-26.

For meditation:

Think about your Christian life in terms of babyhood, childhood, adolescence, young adulthood, middle age, and elderhood. At what stage would you put your current spiritual development? Don't think in terms of how long you've been a Christian or how many Christian activities you're involved in, but rather in terms of how far you've progressed in your reliance on God's Spirit and manifestation of the Spirit's fruit in your life.

Once you have a handle on where you are spiritually, you can begin to see where God wants you to head. Does it seem too far, absolutely unreachable? It should. If it didn't, you wouldn't need God to help you get there. That's what dependence is all about—your depending on God to do that which you couldn't possibly do without Him.

Laughter

I'm often criticized for allowing (or causing) too much laughter in my ministry. I can understand that. In fact, I pray about it a lot. After all, God is holy and sometimes I wonder if laughter is appropriate before holiness. I believe, and have often said, that if you have never stood before God and been afraid, you have probably never stood before God.

Have you read in Isaiah 6 where the prophet encountered God in the temple? That chapter opens with these words: "In the year that King Uzziah died, I saw the Lord seated on a throne, high and exalted" (verse 1). Then the angels shout, "Holy, holy, holy is the LORD Almighty; the whole earth is full of his glory" (verse 3).

Isaiah was doing just fine up to that point. In fact, at the time, he was involved in church work, doing what people do in church (probably picking up the bulletins from the first service), when the real God of the universe came into the temple. It shattered every preconceived idea Isaiah ever had about God. His response was what yours or mine would have been. He cried out, "Woe to me! . . . I am ruined! For I am a man of unclean lips, and I live among a people of unclean lips, and my eyes have seen the King, the LORD Almighty" (verse 5).

If Isaiah had laughed, it would have been highly inappropriate. When people complain about the laughter, I understand their complaint. God, after all, is God, and His awesomeness and power ought to solicit something other than the superficial laughter of His people. And then I start laughing. I don't mean to. It just comes out. I start thinking about Him and all that He has done, and sometimes I can't stifle the chuckles. I've apologized a hundred times. I've tried—God knows I've tried—to be more serious and clergy-like, but I just can't do it. Maybe it's just the natural, nervous laughter that happens when one is frightened. Maybe things are funnier in a serious setting like church or a religious radio broadcast. It could be that the pressure is finally getting to me and my laughter is preceding the words, "They're coming to take me away."

But I don't think so. In fact, I think there's much more laughter in this thing called Christianity than I ever thought. Whether or not you hear that laughter depends on which side of God you find yourself.

For instance, when Isaiah first met God, not only was the experience one where laughter would not have been appropriate, the message Isaiah was given was not for joking either. He received a message of judgment. He was charged to call the people to repentance.

But after the sorrow and the repentance, a veritable flood of laughter rushes out: "and the ransomed of the LORD will return. They will enter Zion with singing; everlasting joy will crown their heads. Gladness and joy will overtake them, and sorrow and sighing will flee away" (35:10). And then, almost as if we didn't get the message the first time, he says it again several chapters later: "The ransomed of the LORD will return. They will enter Zion with singing; everlasting joy will crown their heads. Gladness and joy will overtake them, and sorrow and sighing will flee away" (51:11). When the people of God have been redeemed, God commands them, "Burst into songs of joy together, you ruins of Jerusalem, for the LORD has comforted his people, he has redeemed Jerusalem" (52:9).

In that wonderful passage where Isaiah proclaims the work of Messiah (as well as his own) and from which Jesus quoted in reference to Himself, there is a great statement about the proclamation that comes from the throne of grace:

> The Spirit of the Sovereign LORD is on me, because the LORD has anointed me to preach good news to the poor. He has sent me to bind up the brokenhearted, to proclaim freedom for the captives and release from darkness for the prisoners, to proclaim the year of the LORD's favor . . . to comfort all who mourn, and provide for those who grieve in Zion—to bestow on them a crown of beauty instead of ashes, the oil of gladness instead of mourning, and a garment of praise instead of a spirit of despair. (61:1-3)

We get a lot of people who write to us at Key Life, telling us that we make them laugh. Sometimes people write to tell me a funny story. Some have said that in their world, our broadcast is the one place where they smile. One listener said, "Steve, don't ever get too serious. We need to laugh. I love what you teach, but I also love the fun you have doing it. It makes the teaching and the living better." Then I started feeling guilty again. I prayed, "Father, you didn't call me to be a comedian. You called me to be a Bible teacher. Forgive me if I'm not taking You seriously. Forgive me if I have made something light out of . . ." That was when my prayer was interrupted. I thought I heard laughter. I checked. Do you know what? I did. It was the laughter of God.

So, I have discovered that one of my ministries is laughter. Not the laughter of derision or cynicism, or the laughter that follows a dirty story, but rather the free, uninhibited laughter of the redeemed. That kind of laughter starts at the throne.

That may not sound like much to you. I didn't think so either until a woman wrote to tell me how she had lost her husband. She described her loneliness and how she felt there was no reason to live on. Then she said, "But when I heard you laugh, I laughed too. I just wanted you to know that it helped a lot."

Heaven knows we have enough sour Christians. There isn't much about the world to inspire laughter. The hurt and pain we experience don't leave much room for humor; there's probably more reason for tears than laughter in most lives. So maybe there's a place for a ministry that doesn't take itself too seriously, that lightens up the landscape a bit. Perhaps that doesn't sound so very important, but I think it really is. God has given His people laughter and that laughter has great healing power.

I recently heard about a man who went to the doctor for his annual physical. The doctor came to him with all the reports and test results and told him, "Mr. Jones, your health is very good. There is no reason why you can't live a completely normal life as long as you don't try to enjoy it."

Don't we sometimes communicate the same message to people? We say, in effect, "Now that you have been forgiven for all your sins and you're sure of Heaven, and now that you have meaning in your life and have found a great power in prayer, you ought to be able to live a normal Christian life—as long as you don't try to enjoy it." Of course, biblical truth is important. Reaching out to those with significant needs is important too. We also need to have an uncompromising, clear, and forceful presentation of truth. But all that doesn't exclude laughter—it includes it, transforms it, sanctifies it, even glorifies it.

204

So let's throw back our heads and laugh. God's infinite riches are ours in Christ. What other reason could we ever need to laugh?

TIME TO DRAW AWAY

——————— ✢ ———————

Read Exodus 15:1-21, 2 Samuel 6.

For meditation:

*Take out some paper and put at the top of it
"Reasons to Laugh." Then begin writing under that
heading what you have from God's hand that's cause
for joy. Keep in mind that all good things come from God,
so if you count your spouse, a friend, your home,
or whatever or whoever else as a source of joy,
understand that God is its ultimate source.
It won't take long before you discover how much
you have to laugh about.*

Praise

Whichen Alan Cameron, the covenantor, was in prison, he was brought the head of his son, Richard, on a platter. At the sight, Cameron fell to the floor. Then, after some time, he stood up and said, "It is the Lord. Good is the will of the Lord."

I don't know if I could have done that. It takes a man or a woman of great faith and commitment to look at great tragedy and recognize the hand of God working out His perfect and loving will. The Bible says that "all things work together for good for those who love God and are called according to His purpose" (Romans 8:28, NKJV). Because of that, the Scriptures conclude we should praise Him in all things (Ephesians 5:20, 1 Thessalonians 5:18). But it's very hard to do that with any conviction when we're faced with great tragedy.

Nevertheless, that's what we're supposed to do. I know that. I prayed about it. He told me that even knowing what I ought to do was great progress and that He was pleased with that. So perhaps, when tragedy strikes next, I'll be able to put that knowledge into practice.

TIME TO DRAW AWAY

——— ❖ ———

Read 2 Samuel 12:1-25, Job 1.

For meditation:

Evil is evil. God never wants us to thank Him for evil
because evil does not come from Him—
only good does (James 1:12-18). On the other hand,
because God is God, He can even bring good results
out of evil's destructive forces.

Have you just gone through a difficult time, perhaps even a tragedy? Take comfort in the fact that God is at work, even now, to bring something good out of it all. For that you can thank Him and maintain your trust in Him.

Appreciation

I read the other day about a little boy who lived in the city. All of his life he had lived in one of the worst sections of a large metropolitan area. One summer an inner-city ministry, with a summer camp in the mountains, took him to the camp for two weeks. He was impressed, and he told his mother so. Here's part of what he wrote his mother: "This is a nice place. It's a place where lots of trees grow and where all kinds of birds fly around uncooked."

You know, most people never appreciate something until they either lose it or never have it. What do you take for granted because it has always been there? Maybe birds or your freedom or your home or your church or your heritage . . . maybe even your family? It's good sometimes to count our blessings. To think of what it would be like to be without those blessings. To be thankful, and then to say so to the One from whom every good and perfect gift comes. Have you done that recently?

TIME TO DRAW AWAY
——— ❖ ———
Read Psalm 107, 1 Timothy 4:1-5.

For meditation:

Get out a piece of paper and write two letters—
one to the Lord and one to someone else for whom you feel
thankful. In those letters express to them how much you
appreciate them and why. Then mail both letters—
the one to God mail through prayer, the other will go just
fine through the regular post office.

Both recipients will be blessed. And so will you.

208

Creative Knowledge

One time, just before presidential candidate Al Smith gave a speech, a heckler yelled out, "Smith, tell them all you know, it won't take long."

"No," Smith replied, "I'll tell all we both know. It won't take any longer."

You know something, the older I get the less I know about God and yet I love Him more. When I was younger, I figured I had Him figured. That, of course, was silly. But then, I was young. Now that I'm older and I've walked with Him longer, I know more about how much greater God is than my thoughts about Him and how much more mysterious His ways really are. And that has led me to trust and love Him even more. I have a banner in my study that means more to me as the years go by. Let me share it with you: "My Father, I don't understand Thee. . . . But I trust Thee."

Yes, I know less but now I love more. That's not a bad exchange.

TIME TO DRAW AWAY
——— ❖ ———
Read Habakkuk 1–3.

For meditation:

Faith contains knowledge, but faith also goes beyond knowledge because faith is a matter of trust more than it's a matter of understanding.

Can you trust God enough to allow Him to work in your life beyond what you know or understand? When you learn to do this, you'll learn to love Him all the more.

Are You an Aquarium Keeper?

Have you ever been so excited about a secret that you had to share it or you would burst right open? Is your relationship to Christ like that? Is it so moving and exciting that you can't wait to tell someone about it? It should be. Evangelism is not an option; it's an incredible opportunity and honor wrapped in a requirement.

So many Christians think that evangelism is just a spiritual form of sales: Instead of marketing a product we're marketing a Person. But that's not right. Evangelism is not selling God. He doesn't need our salesmanship, but He does allow us to be a secondary cause in His plan. In the area of evangelism, God's command is clear: He wants us to share the love, forgiveness, and answer we have found in Christ. Too often, however, that's not what we do. As Dr. Kermit Long has pointed out, rather than being fishers of men, we have become keepers of the aquarium.

Think about your business associates, your neighbors, your fellow students, your friends, your family. If you are going to see them won to Christ, what needs to happen? What role can you play? The Apostle Paul gives us six necessities for true, effective evangelism.

First, true evangelism requires the right *connection*. One of the statements I love from Campus Crusade for Christ is, "Before you talk to people about God, make sure you talk to God about people."

Gypsy Smith, the famous evangelist, was converted as a young boy. When he was growing up among gypsies, there was one strictly enforced rule: It was considered improper for a child ever to speak unless spoken to first. Gypsy Smith had a favorite uncle, Rodney, and wanted very much to witness to him about the love of Christ, but because of this rule, he could never find the opportunity. So he just prayed.

One day his uncle said to him, "Son, how do you account for the fact that the knees of your trousers are worn nearly all the way through?"

Smith replied, "I have worn them through praying for you, Uncle

Rodney. I have been praying that you would become a Christian."

At that point Gypsy Smith's uncle listened to the plan of salvation and received Christ.

Do you want your friends to know Christ? Then you need to pray for them. After all, God is the source of all conversion.

Second, along with the right connection, effective evangelism needs *consecration*.

D. L. Moody used to tell about a wealthy man who loved Christ but who simply did not have the ability to speak to another about Him. So each night Moody was in town, the man would hire a horse-drawn cab and have the driver take him to Moody's meetings. Once there, he would pay the driver for two hours and say to him, "I have now paid you. I want you to go in and listen to Mr. Moody while I stay here and watch your horses."

Nobody ever came to know Christ free. Don't get me wrong. The gospel is free; you don't have to earn it. But it cost God His Son, and it costs us something too. You say you want someone you know to trust in Christ. What price are you willing to pay? Enough to give of your time, money, patience, study . . . whatever? It costs us to reach out.

Third, true evangelism requires *communication*. In Colossians 4:5-6, Paul says that what we present is for others, not for us. When you go fishing, you may not like the worms, but then, they're not for you—they're for the fish.

The world doesn't know what we're talking about when we use words like *born again, justification, vicarious atonement,* or *substitutionary death of Christ on the cross.* We need to learn to express the good news so unbelievers can understand it. As Christians, part of our business is to clearly and accurately communicate what we know about Christ. Can you do that?

Fourth, *anticipation* is another essential to effective evangelism. Colossians 4:5 states, "Be wise in the way you act toward outsiders; make the most of every opportunity." The original Greek literally reads, "Buy back the time." In other words, every time God opens a door, for God's sake walk through it.

One time when Richelieu, a cardinal and statesman in seventeenth-century France, heard of the death of a very elderly and wealthy widow, he was reported to have said, "What a pity. She would have been a fine catch the day before that." It's very important we be just as opportunistic for the cause of Christ. Ask God to make you sensitive when the door is open.

Fifth, true and effective evangelism should always exhibit *consideration*. More people are turned off by the messenger of Christ than by the message of Christ.

There is a young man in my congregation who is now a Christian, married to a Christian girl. He told me, "Steve, first I fell in love with her and then I fell in love with Christ." That's what people are supposed to do. They need to fall in love with us—our compassion, gentleness, and graciousness—and then they will listen to what we have to say.

Sixth, effective evangelism must include *information*. One of the problems with a lot of Christians' presentation of the gospel is that it simply has no content. The gospel becomes a sort of faith in faith or a faith in a nebulous God who loves everybody.

If you take the cross out of the gospel, it is no longer the gospel. If you take sin out of the gospel, it is no longer the gospel. And if you take decision out of the gospel, it is no longer the gospel. The gospel provides specific answers to specific questions and specific needs. In 1 Peter 3:15, Peter writes, "Always be prepared to give an answer to everyone who asks you to give the reason for the hope that you have." And this answer just better have specific content.

A friend of mine who is a member of Jim Baird's church in Jackson told me an incident that Jim shared in one of his recent sermons. Jim recounted that he was playing golf and discovered a drinking fountain on the seventh hole. Because the day was so hot, the golfers were lined up trying to get to the fountain. Just when it was Jim's turn to get a drink, a man jumped in front of him, pushed him out of the way, bent over the fountain, and began to drink. He drank and drank and drank. When, after a long period, the man had finished, he turned to Jim and apologized. "I'm sorry to get in front of you like that. But one time during WWII, my ship was shot out from under me, leaving me to drift for days in the salt water without any fresh water to drink. Now, whenever I get thirsty, I begin to panic. I hope you will forgive me."

When I thought about Jim's story, I thought of those outside the household of faith. They are also drifting on water that can never satisfy their thirst. They need to drink at the fresh eternal springs of the Savior. Jesus said, "Whoever drinks the water I give him will never thirst. Indeed, the water I give him will become in him a spring of water welling up to eternal life" (John 4:14). Unbelievers are drifting on a sea of meaninglessness, guilt, fear, and death. If only we can get them to the clean, fresh water. Then they will drink and drink and drink. Forever.

TIME TO DRAW AWAY
———— ❖ ————

Read Matthew 5:13-16, John 8:1-11.

For meditation:

*What's your commitment to evangelism? Do you love
the lost enough to tell them where true life can be found?
Do you know how to share your faith so others
can understand the gospel?*

*Ask God to open some opportunities to witness for Him.
Then, while you're waiting, take some steps to begin
learning how to evangelize more effectively.
Perhaps reading some books on the topic will help.
You may also want to get together with someone in your
church who evangelizes well.*

*Whatever you do, don't just sit on the good news.
Get it out, let it shine as a light of hope for those
who so desperately need to know how to get out
of the darkness of death.*

Take Off Your Gorilla Suit

He was out of work, out of money, and out of want ads. Desperate, he applied for employment at the county zoo. The zoo keeper told him they didn't really have any work, but he could make a few extra dollars by taking the place of the gorilla who had died at the zoo the day before. Ordinarily, the man would not have done it. But he really needed money, so he accepted the job, put on the gorilla suit, and made his way to the gorilla cage. It really wasn't bad work. All he had to do was eat bananas and swing from a rope. After a while, he began to even like the job.

Then it happened. One day, while the man was swinging on the rope, it broke, depositing him over the fence into the lion cage. He yelled for help as the lion slowly moved toward him. The closer the lion got, the louder he yelled. Finally, the lion came right up to him, nudged him, and said, "Buddy, will you please shut up before we're both out of a job?!"

Are you wearing a gorilla suit? The difference between some Christians and the man in the gorilla outfit is that he was forced into his role, we aren't. And yet, we tend to choose roles for which we're not suited, which leads to much of our misery and frustration.

Have you ever seen Christians who seem to be very pure and very spiritual and yet are very miserable? Their problem is that they are playing a role they were never meant to play. Jesus said, "No one is good—except God alone" (Mark 10:18). When we pretend to be good and pure, we have climbed into a gorilla suit.

Then there are those Christians who feel that everything they say comes from Mount Sinai. They make all sorts of political and social pronouncements as if God Himself had given them a corner on truth. God says, "The heart is more deceitful than all else" (Jeremiah 17:9, NASB). The person who acts as if he or she has a corner on truth has stepped into a gorilla costume.

My point? Almost all frustration and anxiety come from a refusal to be what one is.

Someone has said that every creature fulfills the purpose of its creation except man. Have you ever heard of a dog with ulcers? The reason a dog doesn't get them is because a dog doesn't try to be anything other than a dog. Birds don't try to swim, and fish (other than those designed to do so) don't try to fly. All of creation glorifies God by being that for which it was created. The exception is man.

Man was created to glorify God, to be the one creature who would respond in love to a loving Creator. The psalmist expressed the proper position of man: "Whom have I in heaven but you? And earth has nothing I desire besides you. My flesh and my heart may fail, but God is the strength of my heart and my portion forever" (Psalm 73:25-26). Paul said, "So whether you eat or drink or whatever you do, do it all for the glory of God" (1 Corinthians 10:31).

Allowing your life to praise and glorify God may sound like a rather dull enterprise, but it isn't. If you were created for that purpose (and you were), there will be a coming home—a fulfillment of the reason for your creation. You will taste its sweetness and rightness and enjoy its sense of rest. It will bring a sense of reality that doesn't come from any other source.

Christians are unhappy because they try to play a role for which they were not created. They were created to glorify God. It is the desire to be God, rather than to worship God, that creates an almost unbearable tension in the Christian. An elderly pastor once made an excellent point when he said, "It is very hard to glorify God and yourself at the same time."

So then, take off your gorilla suit. You won't be as hot under the collar. You'll feel better and even look better.

TIME TO DRAW AWAY

❖

Read 1 Chronicles 16:8-36, 2 Corinthians 10:12-18.

For meditation:

Spend some time right now just lifting your voice toward Heaven and praising God. Then commit to Him that today all you say and do will be wrapped around giving Him the glory He so abundantly deserves.

215

If you make this a habit, you'll be surprised
at how fulfilled you'll begin to feel. You see, this is what
you were created for, so when you do it, you'll find a sense
of satisfaction that nothing else in life
can ever give you. So glory on!

The Most Important Thing in the World

A number of months after his wife died of cancer, we had a birthday party for Patrick Arnold, a friend and associate. His time of loss was terribly difficult for all of us, but it was especially devastating for him. In the midst of the laughter of the birthday party, Pat got very serious. Tears welled up in his eyes and he said, "You know, I love you guys. You are a soft place for me, and I don't know what I would have done without you. I just wanted you to know."

Pat has been my pastor for a long time. I have gone to him many times when I simply didn't know where else to go. I have watched Pat for a lot of years, and the most significant thing I've observed is his amazing love.

As you can imagine, Pat's birthday party got quite serious for a while. I don't believe there was a dry eye in the bunch. In the silence of that very poignant moment, I found myself praying quietly, "Lord, make me more like Pat. Give me that kind of love he has."

That hasn't always been my prayer. There was a time when I was a young pastor and didn't believe in much. In those days, if I had prayed, I would have prayed that all repent. I thought then that the main business of the church was to change the unjust social institutions which perpetrated racism and poverty. If that happened, I thought, we would build the kingdom of God on earth. I still have a concern for social justice, and I believe that the church should have a consistent social witness. But that isn't the most important thing.

When I finally became a "Bible-thumping fundamentalist" and saw the importance of the eternal verities of the Christian faith, the main thrust of my ministry became truth as expressed in biblical doctrine. I spent a considerable portion of my time trying to straighten out the false doctrine I saw everywhere. My prayer (I had learned to pray by then) was for God to make the church faithful to the Bible. I still pray that prayer sometimes. The absolute truth of Scripture is still very important to me. But that isn't the most important thing.

217

And then I became very concerned with the task of evangelism. I conducted evangelism seminars around the country, I trained people in the methods of sharing their faith in Christ, and I prayed that God would bring more workers into the fields which were white unto harvest. I still pray that prayer, and I'm still concerned about evangelism. I still believe that the main thrust of the church should be the proclamation of the gospel to the lost. But that isn't the most important thing.

There was a time in my ministry when I thought the empowering of the Holy Spirit should be the most important concern of the people of God. After all, one could work, believe, and evangelize, but if God's Spirit was not empowering the work, the belief, and the evangelism, it would be to no avail. I still pray in the words of the song, "Come, Holy Spirit, revive Thy church again." I still see the necessity of God's Spirit motivating and empowering the people of God. But that isn't the most important thing.

As I get a lot older and a little wiser, I have come to see that the most important thing is love—not the insipid and silly love of the world, but the kind of love demonstrated by Christ on the cross. Paul could write:

If I speak in the tongues of men and of angels, but have not love, I am only a resounding gong or a clanging cymbal. If I have the gift of prophecy and can fathom all mysteries and all knowledge, and if I have a faith that can move mountains, but have not love, I am nothing. If I give all I possess to the poor and surrender my body to the flames, but have not love, I gain nothing.

Love is patient, love is kind. It does not envy, it does not boast, it is not proud. It is not rude, it is not self-seeking, it is not easily angered, it keeps no record of wrongs. Love does not delight in evil but rejoices with the truth. It always protects, always trusts, always hopes, always perseveres.

Love never fails. But where there are prophecies, they will cease; where there are tongues, they will be stilled; where there is knowledge, it will pass away. . . .

And now these three remain: faith, hope and love. But the greatest of these is love. (1 Corinthians 13:1-8,13)

When my brother died, so many people wrote and told me that they were praying for me. And during the more recent scary time with my mother's cancer, people's concern and love meant more than anyone could know.

We live in a time when there are many very harsh voices vying for attention. Hatred, anger, and hostility are the marks of our time. You can even find those ugly marks among the people of God. But you can also find the kind of support from others that has become a soft place for me. And when you find it, or when you give it, you'll understand it is really what Christianity is all about. It's the most important thing in the world.

TIME TO DRAW AWAY

——————— ✛ ———————

Read 1 Samuel 19, Colossians 4:7-15.

For meditation:

The next time you learn of someone who is hurting or who is just in need of a friend, consider what you can do to show love to that person. Pray for them, yes. But don't stop there. As Christ reaches out to you, so you commit to reach out to others, showing them the love of Christ in you.

Come to think of it, if you know of someone who needs love now, don't wait to go to that person. Be loving today . . . and tomorrow . . . and the next day . . . and the day after that. . . . Get the picture?

Humor

I heard a great story the other day.

President George Bush died and went to Heaven and found that it was a wonderful place. The people were friendly, the food was great, and the gold streets were magnificent. But, to the President's consternation, there was one man who simply wouldn't speak to him.

After a rather long time, President Bush decided to fix the relational problem. He went over to the man and said, "Sir, my name is George Bush, and I hope I haven't done something to offend you. I know I'm a Republican, but political differences shouldn't matter here."

The man said, "No, that isn't the problem. My name is Moses, and the last time I talked to a Bush, it cost me forty years in the wilderness."

No point. Just a funny story. Sometimes Christians need to laugh just because something is funny. I prayed about it, and the Lord said it was okay.

TIME TO DRAW AWAY
―――――― ❖ ――――――
Read Genesis 21:1-7, John 2:1-11.

For meditation:

*Did you ever wonder why Jesus chose a wedding feast
to perform His first miracle? And then, His miracle was
to provide more wine so the celebration could keep going?*

*I think Jesus liked parties, and why not? Those who know
the truth and have been so blessed by God
have more reason to celebrate and laugh
than anyone else in the world.*

Have you had any fun lately? Go ahead. He wants you to.

220

Music

My friend John Debrine is a great Bible teacher, but he's also a great song leader. I have been in congregations of three or four thousand when John would lead people in singing "The Lord's Prayer." It has always been magnificent, sounding like a great heavenly choir.

On one of these occasions, there was a man sitting next to me who looked like he had just swallowed a lemon. He refused to sing. I thought, *Here we have a magnificent song and a magnificent choir and one turkey who won't sing.*

People who don't have a song and don't sing are to be pitied. People, however, who have a song and still don't sing are above all to be pitied. Someone has said that birds sing for no other reason than that they have a song. Jesus is the Christian's song, "and let those refuse to sing who never knew our God." The rest of us ought to just belt it out. The songs please God and draw pagans.

TIME TO DRAW AWAY
—————— ❖ ——————
Read Psalm 147, Ephesians 5:18-20.

For meditation:

*One of the purchases you might consider making is
a hymnal. Most Christian bookstores carry them.
You can use a hymnal to learn some of the songs
that express the great truths of the faith,
the emotional swings of the faithful,
and the need of all mankind for God.*

*The Lord put such great stock in singing that he included
150 songs as an entire section in His Word.
These ancient hymns are called Psalms.*

221

*And even if you don't know their melodies,
you can still sing them. Just make up the tune,
then sing the words to the Lord. There is no
music sweeter to His ears.*

Sacrifice

It is said that one time the Roman Emperor Valens sent lavish gifts to Eusebius, the Bishop of Caesarea in the fourth century. The Emperor was trying to get Eusebius to renounce his faith. But Eusebius looked at the gifts and said, "Sir, your gifts may trap children, but we are nourished by the Bible, and are ready to suffer rather than to allow the word of God to be altered."

The Emperor was furious, and he threatened to use torture and execute Eusebius. But again Eusebius stood his ground, telling the Emperor, "He need not fear confiscation, who has nothing to lose; nor banishment, to whom heaven is his only country; nor torments when his body can be destroyed at one blow; nor death, which only can set him free."

What a giant of the faith. I want to pray, "Lord, do it again. Do it again."

TIME TO DRAW AWAY
— ❖ —
Read Daniel 6, Acts 6:8–7:60.

For meditation:

Are you committed to God enough to risk everything for Him, including your life? If not, then He's not your everything—He's only one thing in your life among everything else.

Begin now to make Him your everything. Commit your all to Him, and you will receive His all in return. And His all is infinitely greater than anything you could ever give Him. And they call this sacrifice?

223

Encouragement: Triumph of the Ordinary

An elderly Scottish minister died after serving some thirty-five years as the pastor of a little village church. At his funeral, a man in the village, with tears streaming down his face, said, "Now there is no one left in our village to appreciate the triumphs of ordinary folks."

That man gave his pastor one of the finest compliments a Christian can ever receive. He was saying, "This minister was a cheerleader for his people."

If you're a Christian, you are called to be a cheerleader for your brothers and sisters in Christ. We spend too much time criticizing and throwing rocks at each other, and, God knows, there is a lot of bad stuff in the Body of Christ. However, wouldn't it be nice if someone said to you, "I just want you to know that I'm proud of your faithfulness"? Better, wouldn't it be nice if you said that to a fellow sojourner?

TIME TO DRAW AWAY
❖

Read Matthew 7:1-5, Ephesians 4:29-32.

For meditation:

Do people like to be with you because they find in you a sensitive soul, anxious to listen, slow to speak, and quick to encourage? If not, what is it in you that keeps these qualities from coming forward? Do some internal auditing, then ask the Lord to help you balance the books toward becoming a real encourager.

224

Witness

One time Dr. Harry Ironside was speaking at a street meeting in San Francisco. When he finished speaking, an agnostic handed his business card to Ironside. On it he had written a challenge to debate Ironside the next afternoon on the topic "Agnosticism versus Christianity."

Dr. Ironside read the invitation to the debate and reportedly said aloud to the man and the gathered crowd:

> I accept this challenge on one condition, that my agnostic friend defend the worth of his philosophy by bringing to the debate witnesses who will give testimony to the power of agnosticism to transform human life. I will bring with me one hundred witnesses who will tell of the power of Christ in changing their lives.

As the agnostic waved his hand negatively and walked out of the crowd, everyone began to applaud.

In the face of changed lives, people do applaud. A changed life is always better than mere words.

TIME TO DRAW AWAY
────── ❖ ──────
Read Matthew 7:21-29, James 1:21-27.

For meditation:

Are you a talker or a doer? God wants doers. Then, when they speak, people will listen. Are people listening to you?

CHAPTER SEVEN

GODLY ACTION THAT OVERCOMES

❖

*"I am the Alpha and the Omega,
the Beginning and the End. I will give of the
fountain of the water of life freely to him who thirsts.
He who overcomes shall inherit all things,
and I will be his God and he shall be My son.
But the cowardly, unbelieving, abominable,
murderers, sexually immoral, sorcerers, idolaters,
and all liars shall have their part in the lake
which burns with fire and brimstone,
which is the second death."*

Jesus the Christ
Revelation 21:6-8, NKJV

A Soft Place

There are many lessons to be drawn from the story of Jesus' visit to the home of Mary and Martha as it is recorded in Luke 10, but one I find of particular interest is the fact that even our Lord needed a "soft place" in His life. And this home was that place. It was where He stopped to rest before His ordeal on the cross. What does that say to us? It says that if Jesus needed those soft places and times of rest from the harshness and the pressures of life, then we also need those places and times in our lives.

I believe that one of the most subtle dangers Christians face is the falsehood that commitment precludes soft places. "After all, the world is going to hell in a hand basket! We have a building program to work on. We have plans and programs and things to do for God. We're going to die, and there's so little time. We don't have time for soft places." That's just not true! I believe this account in Luke 10 was included in Scripture so we might know that Jesus Himself needed soft places. And if He needed them, we do too!

Have you ever been in somebody's home where you felt comfortable enough to take your shoes off? Very few people have this gift of hospitality. I travel a lot, and often I stay in people's homes. It can be difficult sometimes because I have to be the "Reverend" and be "spiritual" when I'm in those kinds of homes. But sometimes, in a serendipitous way, I'll come into somebody's home and feel like I can sit down in an easy chair, take my shoes off, and even fall asleep as they talk, and it's okay. That's a very precious gift some Christians have. That's a soft place. It's very rare and very valuable.

Have you ever had a friend with whom you didn't have to pretend? A friend before whom you can weep if you feel like it, or let your strongest emotions show and he or she wouldn't be shocked? That's a soft place too.

Or have you ever given your all, only to find yourself rejected and alone? Then a friend would call and say, "I know it cost you dearly to take that stand, and I know that many people don't understand. But I want you to know that I understand, and I'm praying for you, and I'm standing with you." That's a soft place, and oh, how good it feels.

Our daughter Robin called from college quite often, and it's interesting to notice that when I answered the phone, she said, "Hello, Dad, let me tell you what I learned in philosophy class today." And we talked about her philosophy class for about three minutes. Then she would say, "Is Mom there?" and I'd say, "Yes," and give the phone to Anna. Then, for the next two to three hours, Anna and Robin would be talking. Anna would be laughing and crying and they'd both have a wonderful time. As I watched this phenomenon, I realized that Anna was the soft place in our home, and that alone makes her very valuable.

Now, what am I saying? This: *It's the church's responsibility, corporately and individually, to be a soft place for one another.* And when we cease to be that soft place, then something essential that ought to be present in the church is lost. We're called to be people who create soft places. There are two kinds of people in the world: those who make others great, and those who diminish others. Our business as believers is to create soft places where people can become great.

Are you a soft place for somebody? Or do you diminish them? I've seen Christians do that. A new believer is too excited about discovering Jesus and comes skipping into the church and somebody says, "What are you wearing lipstick for? You can't do that! We're spiritual in this place!" And all of a sudden, the joyous stanza of God's song is stomped into the dirt by someone who didn't understand that the church is supposed to be a soft place for the people of God.

Our Lord needed soft places, and you do, and I do too!

TIME TO DRAW AWAY
— ✤ —
Read 1 Kings 17:8-24, 1 John 3:16-18.

For meditation:

Are you a soft place for someone? Is your home a soft place? Do you have someone who is a soft place for you? All these questions are essential for you to discover if soft places are present in your life. If they aren't, you begin

229

putting them there by becoming a soft place for those around you. Then ask God to bring someone into your life who can be a soft place for you. That's not a selfish request—it's an essential one for living.

Speaking Hard Truths

I was with my friend Fred Smith not too long ago. We were having lunch with a very well-known personality. During lunch, Fred kept contradicting this particular man, correcting him several times. When we were walking away, I asked Fred what he was doing.

"Steve," he replied, "I may be the only friend he has. He has a lot of admirers, a lot of worshipers, and a lot of solicitors, but he doesn't have anybody who will tell him the truth. He knows that I don't want anything from him, and he knows that I'm his friend. I have a gift that very few can give him. I can give him the gift of truth."

Did you ever think that you owed your friends the truth? That's what friends do: They love each other enough to tell each other the truth. That's sometimes painful, and sometimes it causes heartbreak, but it must be done anyway. If you ever lose a friend because you wouldn't hold back the truth, you made a mistake about it being a friendship in the first place.

So go. Tell the truth. Do it with love and compassion and gentleness, but do it. Your friend will come to appreciate you more for it.

TIME TO DRAW AWAY
❖

Read Proverbs 12:17-22, Ephesians 4:25.

For meditation:

Do you have a friend who needs you to speak some truth?
Prayerfully go to that person and tell the truth.
Do it with love and compassion and gentleness, but do it.
If your friend is a true friend, your words may go down
hard, but he or she will come to appreciate you more
for taking the risk and acting in love.

231

Giving

I've heard it said, "Show me your checkbook, and I'll tell you how much you love God." That's probably true.

John Wesley once preached a sermon with three points. "The first," he said, "is make all you can . . ." and an old saint in the front row said, "Amen."

Then Wesley said, "Not only should you make all you can, you ought to save all you can," and the saint in the front row said, "Amen."

Then Wesley added, "Not only should you make all you can and save all you can, you should give all you can," and the saint in the front row said, "Why spoil a good sermon?"

Listen, friend, pagans don't have a reason to give, so giving is up to us, the people of God. On another occasion Wesley said, "Whenever I have money, I give it away quickly lest it burn a hole in my heart." That's good counsel.

TIME TO DRAW AWAY
❖

Read Deuteronomy 15:7-11, 2 Corinthians 9:6-15.

For meditation:

Do you give of your finances regularly, thoughtfully, and sometimes sacrificially? Do you also give of your talents and gifts so others can benefit from what God has provided? It's in giving of ourselves and our possessions that we receive far beyond what we could ever acquire by working to earn and save it. That may sound paradoxical, but it's a truth embedded in the Christian perspective of life. Are you willing to really live by it? Your life will be all the richer if you do. God promises that.

A Lesson in Evangelism

I believe that if you say you're in fellowship with the Father and you don't have a concern for the salvation of anyone else, you're simply not in fellowship with the Father. It's the nature of the Christian to want others to find what he or she has found. Unfortunately, that very desire can hurt the Kingdom of God if it isn't properly channeled and effectively used. As many people are turned away from God's Kingdom by bad witnessing as by no witnessing.

In the account of Jesus and the Samaritan woman, the master Evangelist gives us some very wise lessons in evangelism (John 4:1-42). Our wisdom lies in following His example. So before you read on, read that passage in John that records Jesus' encounter with the Samaritan woman.

First, did you notice that Jesus was sensitive to God's opportunity? He didn't have to create one. From a simple statement of need, that of thirst, Jesus found the opportunity to present the whole counsel of God and to see a brand-new name enter the Book of Life.

I once asked a man who had led hundreds of people to Christ to tell me his secret. "There is no secret," he said. "God opens doors and I walk through them. I just ask the Lord to make me sensitive to open doors."

Last week, every Christian had many opportunities to witness to the name of Christ, but most of us blew it. Your friend who didn't understand why you couldn't play golf last Sunday—did you tell him? Your date who couldn't understand why the evening ended in the living room instead of the bedroom—did you tell him or her? Your neighbor who has asked you repeatedly how she can cope with her husband—did you tell her? If Christians, you and I, were faithful, every evangelist could retire.

Second, note that Jesus did not recognize manmade boundaries. As background to the account, you need to know that there was a standing feud between Jews and Samaritans over the place of worship. Jews didn't even talk to Samaritans. On top of that, a Jewish man simply didn't carry on a conversation with a woman in public. Rabbis didn't have extensive theological discussions with prostitutes either. Jesus ignored these manmade boundaries to share something much more important.

A friend of mine made an observation: People will not share Christ with someone if they feel inferior (socially, economically, or physically) to them. And I've noticed that we often don't share Christ with those to whom we feel superior, either. When we share, if at all, we generally share only with our peers. And that's a shame—indeed, that's a sin. We have the responsibility to share Christ with whomever and whenever God wants us to, and that's that. He opens the doors, yes, but He opens far more doors than we're open to walking through.

The Doyles went to Colombia to speak to the Indians. They went to an old Indian chief who said after hearing their gospel presentation, "Did your fathers know this?"

"Yes, they did," admitted the Doyles.

"Then why did they not come to tell my father?"

Our children may be asked the same question. It just won't wash if we say that they felt superior or inferior, that there was a racial problem, or a problem of geography or language. Manmade boundaries are just that—manmade, not God-made. So we don't have to respect them, especially when something so much greater is at stake.

Third, Jesus did not engage in polemics; He presented the truth: "Yet a time is coming and has now come when the true worshipers will worship the Father in spirit and truth, for they are the kind of worshipers the Father seeks. God is spirit, and his worshipers must worship in spirit and in truth" (John 4:23-24). Jesus had a perfect opportunity to get into a theological argument here, but He didn't.

One of the ways you can recognize unbelievers is to observe the silly things they say about God. Now, you can either point out their silliness or you can point them to Jesus, but you can rarely do both. One of the great problems with Christians is that we get off on peripheral issues, rather than discussing the central issue, which is Jesus Christ. You see, when a man needs medicine, you don't quibble over the color of the pill.

Fourth, Jesus was not in the business of condemnation. John 3:17 teaches, "For God did not send his Son into the world to condemn the world, but to save the world through him."

Superficial Christianity looks at a passage like this and proclaims, "Never judge another person." Well, that's simply not biblical. Within the family (1 Corinthians 6), we are called to judge. I can't be obedient to the Father unless you are obedient to the Father in pointing out my sins and my errors. However, our place is not to judge outside the family of God. If you find a pagan drunk or high or hateful, tell him about Jesus. Don't tell him how bad he is. When God's Spirit is operating on unbelievers, you don't have to convince them how bad they are; they already know it because the Spirit has shown that to them. When God's Spirit is *not* working on a man or a woman, you don't have to convince them how bad they are either; you can't. It is not your place to go around pointing out sin everywhere since you're a sinner too. You are called to present Jesus. The Judge will handle the judging.

Fifth, looking back on the way Jesus dealt with the woman at the well, we can see that His method fit the occasion. "Jesus answered her, 'If you knew the gift of God and who it is that asks you for a drink, you would have asked him and he would have given you living water'" (John 4:10).

I remember the time we visited the Ernest Hemingway's house in Key West. The tour guide was an elderly, earthy lady who was delightful. She had but one problem: Her speech was memorized, causing her to become confused when it was interrupted. Someone said, "She has a record player in her mind. Take the needle off the record and she has a hard time getting it back in the right place!"

A lot of Christians have the same problem. I'm not against memorizing the steps of salvation as evangelistic aids. I just think there's more to the gospel than merely memorizing something and spitting it out. You've got to know the gospel's Source, then you're free to act in obedience to the situation as it's presented to you. As fishers of men and women, we need to understand that there are different kinds of fish that require different kinds of bait. We must be sensitive to those differences.

Finally, note that the truth Jesus gave to this woman was shareable. "Many of the Samaritans from that town believed in him because of the woman's testimony. 'He told me everything I ever did'" (verse 39). If what you have shared with an unbeliever can't be shared by that unbeliever in the next five minutes with another, then you've blown it.

Some of our gospel presentations are so elaborate that when anyone receives Christ it's a miracle. And when they do, the new believers have to go to seminary just to learn how to share their newfound faith.

What Jesus shared was shareable. It was shareable because it was love—the love that changes, satisfies, and cares enough to say enough and no more. But then, if we understood love, the kind of love with which Jesus loved this woman, we wouldn't need advice on how to evangelize. Love is sensitive to God's opportunity; love does not recognize manmade boundaries; Love does not engage in polemics; love is not in the business of condemnation; love adjusts methodology to the occasion; love is shareable. Love takes a worn-out prostitute who is afraid, used, and guilty, and really loves her and gives her a new life, so new that others come to see the source. Love personified is Jesus. Are there any like-minded lovers out there?

TIME TO DRAW AWAY

Read Acts 10, 1 Corinthians 9:19-23.

For meditation:

When was the last time you shared with someone?
How did it go? How did you present the gospel,
handle objections, listen to concerns or fears? Were you
caught up in trying to close a sale or in trying to exemplify
Christ's love to that person?

The next time you share your faith, let love guide your
words and actions. Then watch the difference real love
makes. You'll never share the gospel any other way again.

Putting the Serve Back in Service

"You spend and we'll serve." Though never expressed publicly in those words, that philosophy is rampant throughout our service industries. In a day when some banks and utility companies (to single out a few) are gouging the public, it's no wonder our definition of the word *servant* is somewhat fuzzy. When you consider the outlandish behavior of some of Christianity's most visible "stars," the servant concept becomes distorted to the point of nonrecognition.

Just what is a servant, and what is this task of servanthood Jesus calls us to in John 13? How can you and I put the serve back in servanthood?

The answer begins with love. When you came to Christ, you received more than salvation—you received love. That love is to be spread around with no strings attached. And when that happens, servanthood begins.

Some natives in a missionary country regularly traveled fifteen miles out of their way to go to a Christian hospital. Perplexed, the Christian doctor asked them, "Why do you do it? The government hospital is close to you, and the medicine is the same. Why don't you go there?"

The natives answered, "The medicine is the same but the hands are different."

The hands that made the difference were the hands made gentle by the love of Christ.

Second, the context of the servant is power. It's no big deal to wash feet. The big deal is to see who washed the feet.

While observing a nurse ministering to the sick and dying of WWII, a reporter told her, "Sister, I wouldn't do that for a million dollars."

"Brother," she replied, "I wouldn't either."

There was power in her servanthood because she was saying, "I don't have to be a servant. I have *chosen* to be a servant."

You are a child and representative of the King. When God's

representative washes dirty feet or binds up wounds, that is really something! Christian servanthood is only meaningful in the context of power and authority. If you haven't found out who you are, don't go and serve. It will be wasted.

Third, there is a contrast in servanthood. Look at John 13:8: "'No,' said Peter [to Jesus], 'you shall never wash my feet.'" Peter was expressing shock at the contrast between the world's leaders and God's Leader. God's Leader was washing feet; the world's leaders would never do that.

When was the last time you allowed someone to go ahead of you in line? When was the last time you smiled when someone insulted you? When was the last time you loved rather than demanded? That's the demeanor of the disciple of Jesus; a shocking inclination to servanthood, not a common-pack shout for your rights. When you say, "It's not fair," it shows that you haven't understood the contrast of the servant. If things were fair, you would have never known Him.

Finally, there is conformity in servanthood. In John 13:12-16, Jesus gives us an example to follow: "When he had finished washing their feet, he put on his clothes and returned to his place. 'Do you understand what I have done for you? . . . Now that I, your Lord and Teacher, have washed your feet, you also should wash one another's feet.'" Jesus was a model. That's what you are supposed to be.

Do you want to know how to be a servant? Look at Jesus. Do you want to know how to love? Look at Jesus. Do you want to know how to live? Look at Jesus. I thank God for the model He gave us in Jesus. It is always right. And if we look at His example long enough and hard enough, there's no question that we'll start putting the *serve* back into servanthood.

TIME TO DRAW AWAY
———— ✤ ————

Read Galatians 5:13-14, 1 Peter 4:7-11.

For meditation:

What kind of servant are you? Do you serve with humility, concern, gentleness, unconditional love? Or do you let others know how much they should appreciate what you do for them, do you lord your service over others, using it to manipulate them? The closer your model of servanthood comes to Jesus, the more your serve will be like His. How are you doing?

Planning and Preparation

Poor preparation and planning can cause a major disaster at an airport, on a highway, in a business, in a marriage, in a family . . . virtually anywhere in life. So I'm glad the Bible has a lot to say about this topic.

The writer of Proverbs says, "Go to the ant, you sluggard; consider its ways and be wise! . . . A little sleep, a little slumber, a little folding of the hands to rest—and poverty will come upon you like a bandit and scarcity like an armed man" (Proverbs 6:6,10-11).

Jesus talked about the wedding guest who came to the wedding party without the proper dress (Matthew 22), the fig tree that didn't have fruit (Matthew 24), and the foolish virgins who forgot to bring oil (Matthew 25). Paul admonished the Ephesians to be "strong in the Lord and in his mighty power. Put on the full armor of God so that you can take your stand against the devil's schemes" (Ephesians 6:10-11).

We have all seen those roadside signs with the Scripture from Amos 4, "Prepare to Meet Thy God." The pagans laugh, the Christians are a little embarrassed, and the neighbors have learned to overlook them, but the message is one we all need to consider. Someday we will meet God, and if you never prepare for anything else, you dare not face that meeting without some sort of preparation.

I have often said to congregations, "This is the real world, the community of truth. We are here to prepare to go out into the unreal world. If you know that, you will be prepared." One of the great things about being a Christian is the reality with which we are confronted. In other words, we know the truth, and once one knows the truth, one can prepare.

For instance, we know the truth about the nature of human beings: They are evil with a proclivity for good and not, as the pagans think, good with a proclivity for evil. That is why Christians always lock their doors, keep close watch on the school system, and never trust the politicians.

Another example: We know the truth about the way the universe

240

works. The law of God isn't the method whereby God makes us unhappy; rather, it's a road map giving us the location of the danger zones. That's why Christians are generally more balanced and happy than pagans. As we walk through the mine fields, we know where the mines are.

Or consider this one: We know the truth about the fallen world. The pagans are always looking for the impossible—a perfect and happy situation. They will never find it and therefore waste considerable time looking for it. We know better. We know that here we have no permanent city. We know that we aren't home yet. We realize that nothing is perfectible this side of Heaven.

Here's another: Christians have learned to face the fact of death. Pagans ignore it, and when they can't ignore it, they cover it up with clichés and flowers. We know that the death statistic is one out of one, and that nobody is going to get out of this thing alive. Therefore, with the psalmist, we know to number our days, that we might gain a heart of wisdom.

Yet another, for instance: Christians know there's a God and that nobody is exempt from checking in when the show is over. Pagans think they will explain things to God and that He will understand, pat them on the back, and say, "It's cool." Christians know better. We know that unless we get in on the coattails of Jesus, we aren't going to make it.

And another: Christians know how history is going to end, so we govern ourselves accordingly. Pagans figure that history will always continue with new story lines and new actors. But we can convey to pagans what C. S. Lewis is reported to have said: "When Christ returns, how awful to know that all of it was true, and that it is too late to do anything about it."

TIME TO DRAW AWAY
————— ❖ —————
Read Romans 14:7-13, 2 Corinthians 5:9-11.

For meditation:

If you see the value of preparing and planning in this life for what you would like to do, how much more important are preparation and planning for life beyond the grave.

241

Do you live your life with your ultimate future in mind? If not, think about what you need to start doing today to make your heavenly future so much more enjoyable. Believe me, this kind of approach to your next life will have a profound impact on the quality of your life in the here and now. You'll see. Trust me. But trust Him mostly.

Growing in Christ, Growing in Grace

A cowboy and an Indian were riding across the plain heading for town. All the cowboy could talk about was food. "When I get into town, I'm goin' to get the biggest steak I can find and I'm goin' to chow down." The Indian didn't respond.

Finally, the cowboy asked, "Aren't you hungry?"

"No," said the Indian.

When they got into town and ordered a meal, the Indian ate twice as much as the cowboy. The cowboy said, "Out on the plain you said you weren't hungry."

The Indian replied, "Not wise to be hungry then. No food."

A lot of Christians are like that. They have learned to accept their state simply because they think they have no alternative. In other words, he or she thinks, *It isn't wise for me to think that I'm going to be better because, given my sinful nature, there's no way I can ever get better.* At that point, Christians give up and give in. It's easy to get cynical if you've ever tried to be good.

The truth is, growth is hard but it is also possible. Peter, who had as much trouble growing as any Christian who has ever lived, gives us some important teaching in 2 Peter 1:3-11 about growth. Let's check it out.

Peter tells us the *resource* of growth. His divine power has given us everything we need "for life and godliness" (verse 3). The desire you have to be better didn't come from you—it came from God. In God's economy, there's a correlation between aspiration and realization. If God has given you a desire, He will give you a way. If He doesn't give you a way, He didn't give you the desire.

Christ is the motivating force behind growth. The promises He gives are the assurance that it won't be a waste of your time. Do you know people who have run out of steam? Let me tell you. They are the ones who are trying to be good so everyone will notice; the ones who are trying to be good because Christians are supposed to be good; the

243

ones who are trying to be good because it is proper. I've been all three of those. I thought, given my nature, that in getting rid of those three motivations, I wouldn't want to be good. But do you know something? I still desperately want to be good. That desire comes from the throne of grace. Discouragement is the bane of every Christian. But nevertheless, I keep on trying, working, and pushing. Why? I don't know why. There is just something in me that won't let go.

Second, take a look at the *road* of growth. The process of sanctification is just that, a process. It's a road, where with each step you get closer to the goal.The road starts with faith as a gift. Proper faith leads to virtue. When you have virtue, you then have the possibility of knowledge; as God works, you have a curiosity about Him. Once you have attained knowledge, you can proceed to self-control. As you take the first step, God will take the second step. By the third step, you will know God actually took the first step. When self-control is increasingly a reality in your life, you'll find that you can add perseverance. Perseverance leads to godliness, the fact that you're better today than you were yesterday. Godliness leads to brotherly kindness; God will give you the gasoline for loving your brothers and sisters in Christ. Finally, brotherly kindness leads to love, which is the capstone of all that God is doing in your life.

Love is what growth is all about. And sometimes, in our love, we discover family members we didn't know before.

Third, observe the *ramifications* of growth. "For if you possess these qualities in increasing measure, they will keep you from being ineffective and unproductive in your knowledge of our Lord Jesus Christ. . . . Therefore, my brothers, be all the more eager to make your calling and election sure" (verses 8,10). This shows three benefits of growth: Your faith will work in a very practical way; there is fruit (your life will be effective and will count); and you'll find that you will increasingly become good.

A friend of mine has a grandson who is always being reprimanded at school. (I can identify with that!) My friend asked his grandson why he couldn't be good, and he answered, "Granddaddy, it's not that I can't be good. I can't be good enough long enough."

Peter says that, as you grow in Christ, your life will become a habit of effectiveness. You won't always know how effective you have been, but God will use you in a wonderful way.

Fourth, notice the *repudiation* of growth. "But if anyone does not have them, he is nearsighted and blind, and has forgotten that he has been cleansed from his past sins" (verse 9). Peter's description of the people who refuse to grow is relatively mild. He doesn't say, "You will burn in hell and I'll be glad." He doesn't say, "You will get the fever and die." Rather he says, "You will be shortsighted and blind." In other words, looking back over your life, you will say with great regret, "It could have been different, and it would have been better if it had been different."

There is no greater feeling in the world than living a life that is pleasing to God. Fictional evil is attractive and fictional good is bland, but in real life, the situation is just the opposite. Following Christ is the most exciting thing in the world.

Sometimes I ask God to cause me to remember the way it really was. I can remember, just starting out in Boston, coming back to my apartment and crying like a baby. I can remember in high school feeling lonely and outcast. I can remember the meaninglessness I felt as I read Albert Camus. I can remember the time I thought to myself, *Is this all there is?* The principle is this: If you remember, you will do it right.

Quincy, "the Wonder Dog," wants more than anything in the world to please me. He wants to please me a lot, but he forgets. Training a dog is not training him in love, it is reminding him. People are like that, too.

Finally, don't miss the *reward* of growth: "For if you do these things, you will never fall, and you will receive a rich welcome into the eternal kingdom of our Lord and Savior Jesus Christ" (verses 10-11). This seems to teach that there are different places in Heaven. In other words, if you find only a shack for you to live in, that will be all the building material you sent ahead of you.

More important than that, though, is the glorious hope of Heaven. The older I get, the more I see wrong with the earth. I'm afraid of death now, but I'm less afraid of it than I used to be. By the time it gets to the point where I simply won't be able to stand the pain, the disease, the hurt, the fear, and the corruption, I'll be ready for a better place—my heavenly home. In the words of C. S. Lewis, "Aim at heaven and you will get earth thrown in. Aim at earth and you will get neither."

TIME TO DRAW AWAY

———— ✤ ————

Read 1 Corinthians 14:20, 2 Peter 3:14-18.

For meditation:

When you were a kid, your parents probably had a growth chart in your room to check how tall you had grown. Every once in a while, you'd stand up next to that chart and your parents would check your height.

As a child of God, He has a growth chart that He always checks you against. The chart is Christ— His character, His actions, His tongue control, His compassion, His understanding. When was the last time you stood next to that chart and listened to the Lord tell you how your growth rate is coming along?

Don't wait any longer. Do it now, in prayer. Then listen carefully. God will tell you how you're doing and what you can do to keep growing. He's a loving parent. He'll steer you right.

Nostalgia

J ohn Gardner said once, "It's never wise to be nostalgic about something unless you are absolutely certain that it won't happen again." In other words, because of our selective memories, the past is never the way we remember it. We tend to forget the bad and magnify the good.

Moreover, nostalgia is like going into a bakery when you are on a diet. The bakery smells good, but you can't eat any of it. Don't get me wrong. Memories are good. But hope is better. Paul quoted Isaiah, saying that the "Eye has not seen, nor ear heard, nor have entered into the heart of man the things which God has prepared for those who love Him" (1 Corinthians 2:9, NKJV).

I must admit that sometimes I am nostalgic, but more and more I'm finding that I'm hopeful. If you're a Christian, the future is going to be a lot better than the past, no matter how good the past has been. And that's a fact.

TIME TO DRAW AWAY
——— ❖ ———
Read Isaiah 65:17-19, Revelation 21:1–22:5.

For meditation:

Remembering can be enjoyable or painful,
and looking ahead can be exciting or scary. But when you
begin to imagine all the great things God has in store
for those who are His sons and daughters in Christ,
well . . . your imagination can't even begin to grasp it all.

But take some time now to try. Using the biblical texts
cited for your reading as guides, try to imagine what
a world of uninterrupted bliss will be like. Try to imagine
a world without pain, without suffering,

247

without malice of any kind, where everyone is kind, compassionate, caring, totally unselfish, and completely satisfied all the time. Then remember, regardless of how great your picture of that new world is, it still won't come close to what it will really be like. Now that's something to hope for. Who needs nostalgia when you can look forward to such an incredible world?

Obedience Has a Cost

At the entrance to a small inn in a town in Vermont, there's a regulation-size post office box. But, instead of having posted the usual hours of collection notice, the following message has been posted: "Neither rain nor snow nor gloom of night shall stay us from delivering this mail to the post office across the street at least once a day . . . weather permitting and providing there is enough mail in this box to make the trip worthwhile." A lot of Christians are that way about their obedience. As long as it's convenient, they'll be obedient.

The Bible says that we should look to Jesus, "who . . . endured the cross, despising the shame" (Hebrews 12:2, NKJV). If it had been convenient, His sacrifice would have been far less valuable.

When you're obedient and it doesn't cost you anything, that's nice. When you're obedient and it costs, God is pleased. His pleasure is worth the inconvenience. What Jesus accomplished on the cross for us proves that.

TIME TO DRAW AWAY
— ✤ —
Read Genesis 39, Luke 14:25-33, 1 Peter 2:18-24.

For meditation:

*When was the last time your obedience led to real
sacrifice? Following Christ will not always be hard,
but if you never really sense that the cost
of your obedience is becoming greater,
perhaps you're just coasting. Ask Him about it.
He'll let you know how things really stand.*

249

Contentment

During his many appearances in summer stock theater in the role of Tevye in "Fiddler on the Roof," actor Robert Merrill learned to expect the unexpected. One night, Tevye's horse had lost a shoe, and Merrill, playing the character, implored God to give him a replacement. At that point, a small, spotted dog walked onto the stage. The audience started laughing, and Merrill bowed his head and prayed, "Oh, Lord, would you try again?"

When God grants us answers to our prayers, we often wish he would try again. Dissatisfied with His answers, we become ungrateful and slap the hand that's trying to feed us only that which is good. When you think about it, that's pretty ridiculous.

We would enjoy much greater peace and satisfaction in life if we would stop asking the Lord to try again and accept what, in His love and mercy, He decides to give. Someone has said that happiness does not consist in getting what you want but in wanting what you get. For the Christian, we need to modify that a bit: Happiness consists in being thankful for what God graciously gives. As the Apostle Paul put it, "I have learned in whatever state I am, to be content" (Philippians 4:11, NKJV).

TIME TO DRAW AWAY
— ❖ —

Read Psalm 103, Philippians 4:11-13.

For meditation:

*Rather than consider what more God might do for you,
take some time to thank Him for what he has already done
for you. Consider what He has done for you
in salvation, creation, spiritual growth, relationships,
finances, and so on.*

250

Then begin thanking Him now for what He has planned for your future, both in this life and in the life to come.

Just give Him praise. He certainly deserves it.

Old Thoughts and New Beginnings

W̄e all know that there's really no difference between December 31 and January 1; nevertheless, it's inevitable when we stand at the end of an old year and look into a new one that we evaluate and plan.

I'm not very big on New Year's resolutions. I already have enough guilt without adding to it by resolving to do something that I probably won't ever do. In fact, the only New Year's resolution that I have made the past few years, and the only one I have kept faithfully, is the resolution that I will not make New Year's resolutions.

Michel Quoist, the late French priest, has a wonderful prayer of confession in which, after a fairly detailed acknowledgment of his sin, prays:

> Lord, don't look at me like that,
>   For I am naked,
>   I am dirty,
>   I am down,
>   Shattered,
>   With no strength left.
>   I dare make no more promises,
>   I can only lie bowed before you.

I understand that. January promises broken in February produce guilt in March, and I already have enough of that. As I've said, the grandson of a friend of mine says, "Granddaddy, I can be good. I just can't be good enough long enough." And a year of good is a whole lot of good.

I have a friend who was active in a church I served near Boston. He was one of the finest and most godly men I have ever known. One day we were sitting around talking, and out of the blue, he started crying. For the next hour I listened to a surprising confession from a man who, in a missions conference nearly thirty-five years before, had promised that he would go on the mission field. Never mind that he had been prevented from that because of responsibilities to his parents; never mind that he had made an amazing contribution physically and financially to his church; never mind that he had been a faithful witness to unbelievers, leading a number of his friends to Christ; never mind that he had been a good father and husband; never mind that he had faithfully followed Christ in all of his business dealings . . . he had made a resolution before God and had not fulfilled it.

We talked about forgiveness. I told him that God was not a policeman but his Father. I told him that, if I could understand, I was sure God, whose understanding and compassion were far greater than mine, could understand.

We talked about how he had not surprised God. We talked about God's sovereignty over his life and the circumstances of his life.

Our talk helped some, but I don't think he ever felt good about himself and his relationship with the Lord.

Then I got the message that my friend had died. I was sad because I loved him a lot, but I was also relieved. I prayed about him, and the Father told me He would tell my friend what I had told him so many years before about forgiveness and love. *Only now,* I thought, *he will believe it, and for the first time in a long time, he will laugh as one who finally understands that the ways of God toward His own are the ways of grace and love.*

That's a "long way around the barn" to say that I'm weary of New Year's resolutions. Not only that, I'm afraid of New Year's resolutions. Notice what James says:

> Come now, you who say, "Today or tomorrow we will go to such and such a city, spend a year there, buy and sell, and make a profit"; whereas you do not know what will happen tomorrow. For what is your life? It is even a vapor that appears for a little time and then vanishes away. Instead you ought to say, "If the Lord wills, we shall live and do this or that." But now you boast in your arrogance. All such boasting is evil. (James 4:13-16, NKJV)

It's taken a long time for me to learn that. The priest who said that when he was a young man he prayed to win the world to Christ, in middle age prayed to win a few, and as an old man prayed he would

253

not lose too many, understood. He understood that resolutions are often poor imitations of obedience, and that they are often reflections of sinful pride in one's own ability to accomplish what needs to be resolved.

Does that mean I don't have any desires for the beginning of a new year? Now that's a different question altogether. The New Year's holiday is a good time to remind myself that the Father is always pleased when the desires of my heart conform with the desires of His.

I desire that I love Him more and serve Him better. I desire to do what is pleasing in His sight. I desire to witness more clearly with my words, my life, and my love to those who don't know Him. I desire to be less critical and more loving. I desire to be a better husband and father (and now, father-in-law). In short, I desire to live my life in such a way as to be willing to sell the family parrot to the town gossip.

The Father told me that it was okay not to make resolutions as long as my desires were proper. My desires please Him. He told me, however, that He was never quite satisfied with the way I kept my resolutions anyway.

In fact, He has only been satisfied once. That was when His Son died on a cross. Jesus' resolution to save His people was kept absolutely. That's why my resolution keeping is of no value to God. That Jesus kept His is all that really matters. Because He did, I'm covered, and I'm getting better.

When we get home, all our God-pleasing resolutions and desires will be completely fulfilled, for then "we shall be like him" (1 John 3:2). See you then.

TIME TO DRAW AWAY
——————— ❖ ———————
Read Psalm 15, John 8:28-29.

For meditation:

How well do your desires match the Lord's?
Take an inventory of what you really want, then compare
your list to what you know God wants. Do you have any
mismatched desires? If so, talk to Him about that.
Ask Him to help you refocus your wants so that in all you
do, you'll be pleasing to Him. That's a prayer He'll
answer affirmatively.

Steve Brown's voice, humor, and insight have become familiar to thousands who listen to Steve daily on Key Life radio network. In addition, he cohosts with Tony Campolo the TV program *Hashing It Out,* broadcast on the Faith and Values Channel.

Steve was a Presbyterian pastor for many years before joining the faculty of Reformed Theological Seminary in Orlando, where he teaches seminarians how to preach. He has written more than ten books (see page 2 for a list), and he has contributed articles to such magazines as *Decision* and *Leadership.*

Steve is one of twenty-six members of the board of directors of *Christianity Today.*